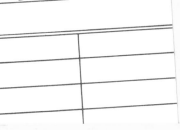

CONSULTING EDITOR:
DAVID PORTER

ADVISERS:

DR. BRUCE METZGER
Princeton Theological Seminary

DR. RUTH ZIELENZIGER
Jewish Theological Seminary,
Melton Research Center, New York

LAURIE ROSENBERG
Board of Deputies of British Jews

CANON DAVID ATKINSON
Southwark Cathedral, London, England

THE REVEREND VERA SINTON
Wycliffe Hall, Oxford, England

DR. JANET AJZENSTAT
DR. SAMUEL AJZENSTAT
McMaster University, Hamilton, Ontario

KINGFISHER
a Houghton Mifflin Company imprint
222 Berkeley Street
Boston, Massachusetts 02116
www.houghtonmifflinbooks.com

First published as *The Kingfisher Children's Bible* in 1993
New edition published by Kingfisher in 1998
This edition first published by Kingfisher in 2003

2 4 6 8 10 9 7 5 3 1

Text copyright © Ann Pilling 1993
Illustrations copyright © Kady MacDonald Denton 1993

All rights reserved under International
and Pan-American Copyright Conventions

LIBRARY OF CONGRESS CATALOGING-IN-PUBLICATION DATA
has been applied for.

ISBN 0-7534-5626-5

Printed in Taiwan

1TR/0503/SHE/PIC/158MA

QUOTATIONS
The author has included quotations from the King James Bible to give readers an idea of the beauty of this
long-established and well-loved translation, and from the New International Version for the compelling clarity of modern
renderings. These appear in italics. For all biblical quotations the author and publishers gratefully acknowledge permission to
reproduce the following copyright material:

The Kingfisher
Book of
BIBLE
STORIES

Retold by Ann Pilling

Illustrated by

Kady MacDonald Denton

KINGFISHER

BOSTON

CONTENTS

THE OLD TESTAMENT

THE NEW TESTAMENT

The Old Testament

בראשית

HOW GOD MADE
THE WORLD

Genesis 1–2

In the beginning God made the heaven
and the earth. But at first the earth was
shapeless and empty, and everything was
covered with thick darkness.

Then God said, "Let there be light!"

And there was light. God saw that it
was good, so he separated it from the
darkness. He called the light "day" and
the darkness "night."

Then God made the sky, stretching it
out over the earth like a great tent, and he
gathered the waters together in one place
so that dry land appeared. On this land he
set plants and trees growing, and it all
seemed very good.

Then lights were put in the sky like
great lamps—the sun, the moon, and the
stars—to mark the seasons and to make
night and day.

Into the sea God put all kinds of fish, and birds to fly above them in the air.

"Multiply," he said to them all, "and fill this land of mine with young."

Then he said, "Let the dry land be filled with animals, with those that walk and creep and jump and run." And it all seemed very good.

At last God said, "Let us make man in our own image and likeness." So mankind was made:

In the image of God created he him; male and female created he them.

And the human creatures he had made were special, because they were like God.

They were put in charge of all the things that now filled the marvelous new world. And God blessed them.

"Rule over the earth and its creatures," he said. "They are for you."

Then God looked all around and saw that his creation was very good indeed. It had taken six long days to make it, so on the seventh day he rested.

That is why the seventh day of the week is a holy day, because it is when God rested from all his work.

11

ADAM AND EVE

Genesis 2–3

The man that God made was named Adam and for him, in a place called Eden, he planted a most beautiful garden. It had four great rivers flowing from it, and flowers and trees of every kind. Two trees were special, the tree of life and the tree of the knowledge of good and evil, which grew right in the middle.

"You may eat fruit from any of the trees," God said, "except from the tree of the knowledge of good and evil. If you do that, you will die."

So Adam lived in Eden, ruling over its animals and giving them all names. But he was lonely, so God made a woman to live with him and share the garden. Her name was Eve.

One day a cunning creature came slinking by and said to her slyly, "Did God really tell you not to eat from any of the trees in the garden?"

"No," Eve answered, "only from the tree in the middle of the garden, the tree of the knowledge of good and evil. If we eat its fruit we shall die."

"That is not true," the creature told her. "You will not die. God only said that because he knows that if you eat from it you will become like him, knowing both good and evil."

Then Eve, seeing how lovely the fruit was, and wanting to be wise like God, stretched out her hand, took it, and ate. And when Adam came he ate also.

In the cool of the evening God walked in his garden and came looking for them, but, knowing they were naked, they were ashamed and had hidden away. He called out to them and said, "Adam, Eve, did you eat fruit from the forbidden tree?"

"Eve gave it to me," answered the man.

"But it was that creature's fault," the woman explained. "He tricked me."

Then God said to the creature, "You will be punished for what you have done. From now on you will be a snake, which cannot walk upright but only crawls along the ground, and you shall eat nothing but

dust." And the wretched snake slithered away.

Then God turned to Adam and Eve. "Now that you have eaten of my tree you must leave this garden and live in the world. From now on you must work, tilling the stony soil until it produces enough food for you to eat." And they went sadly away.

Then God thought, "What if they should now reach out and taste from the tree of life? Then they would live forever."

So when he had cast them out of Eden he put an angel there, and a flaming sword that turned this way and that, to guard the tree of life.

CAIN AND ABEL: THE FIRST MURDER

Genesis 4

Eve had two sons. Their names were Cain and Abel. Abel was a keeper of sheep, but Cain tilled the ground for food.

When his crops ripened Cain offered them to God. Abel offered some first-born lambs. God looked with favor on Abel's offering, but he did not look on Cain's with any favor at all.

Cain was jealous. He said to Abel, "Let us go out to the field," and when they reached it he killed him.

Then the Lord God said, "Where is your brother, Abel?"

"I do not know," Cain answered. "Am I my brother's keeper?"

God said, "What have you done? Your brother's blood cries out to me from the ground. From now on you will be cursed. You will wander all over the earth and you will find no rest."

Cain said, "But I will be killed by the first person who sets eyes upon me."

"No," said God. "If anyone kills you he will be punished seven times over." And he put a mark on him, so that nobody would touch him.

Then Cain went away from the presence of the Lord, to the east of Eden, into the Land of Nod, the "wandering land."

NOAH AND THE FLOOD

Genesis 6–9

Noah was a good man and walked with God, but the rest of the people had become very wicked. God was sad, but he was angry too, so he decided to bring a great flood upon the earth. But he wanted to save Noah and his family.

"You must build a huge wooden boat," God told him, "an ark. You must make it long and wide and tall, and paint it with tar so that the water can't get in. When it is finished you and your family must go inside the ark, and you must take with you a pair of all the animals in my creation, so that when the flood has gone down they can have young, to fill the earth again."

So Noah and his wife, and their three sons, Shem, Ham, and Japheth, set to work and built an enormous boat, exactly as God had said. When it was finished the animals came in, two by two: great lumbering elephants and long-necked giraffes, prickly porcupines and nervous little mice. In through the windows flew birds of every kind: sparrows and thrushes, the raven and the turtle dove. When everything was safe inside, God shut up all the doors and windows very tight. Then the rain came.

It rained for forty days without stopping, and the whole earth turned into one enormous sea. Everything on earth was swept away and drowned, all except Noah and his family and his animals, snug and warm inside the great big boat.

The flood waters churned and bubbled and raged but God did not forget Noah, and at last he made a huge wind that blew across the earth.

Little by little it stopped raining altogether, the floods began to go down, and Noah's ark came to rest on top of Mount Ararat.

When all was calm, Noah opened a window and sent out a raven to see what was happening. But the raven did not return. Then twice he sent a dove. The second time it came back with a fresh green olive leaf in its beak. Then Noah knew that the flood was really over.

When he came out of the boat he built an altar to God, and burned incense upon it as a sacrifice to thank him for sparing their lives. Then God blessed Noah and his sons.

"I promise never to destroy my creation again," he told Noah. While the earth remains, seedtime and harvest, cold and heat, summer and winter, day and night, shall not cease."

As a special sign he put a rainbow in the sky.

"Whenever I see it," he said, "I shall remember my promise."

So Noah and his family and all the animals went back safely into the world and had children, so that the earth was full of living creatures, just as it had been before.

THE TOWER OF BABEL

Genesis 11

After the flood Noah became a farmer and planted vines. Shem, Ham, and Japheth had many sons, and soon there were people living all over the face of the earth. But although there were many people, they all spoke one language.

As one group of people journeyed, they came to a plain in the land of Shinar, and they settled there.

Then they said to one another, "Let us make bricks, let us bake them very hard." So they did. They were building a city, and they wanted it to last forever. "Let us build ourselves a tower too," they said, "a tower that reaches up to the heavens, so that we can make a name for ourselves. Otherwise we shall be scattered to the four corners of the earth."

But God came down to look at the city, and at the tower that mortal men were building, and he said, "If these people, who all speak the same language, can do this, what else will they do? From now on, nothing they set their minds to will be beyond their grasp. Let us go down and mix up their speech, so that they do not understand each other."

So before the city and its tower were finished God scattered the people of Shinar. The place where they had built their tower was called Babel. They had been scattered by the very thing they had built to keep them all together, and now they spoke in different tongues. It was nothing but a babble.

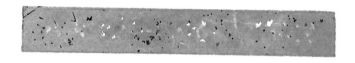

ABRAM AND LOT

Genesis 12–13

Abram, the son of Terah, heard the voice of God speaking to him: "Leave your country," the Lord said. "Leave your family and your father's house and go to a land that I will show you. And in you shall all the families of the earth be blessed."

Abram obeyed God, and set off with his wife, Sarai, and his nephew, Lot. They were traveling toward the land of Canaan. When they reached Shechem, God appeared to Abram and said, "I will give this land to your descendants."

Abram traveled on, but he doubted that this could ever come true. Sarai was too old to have children now.

So, in a vision, God came to him. "I am your shield and your very great reward," he said.

Then he led him outside and said, "Look at the stars. You will have as many descendants as these."

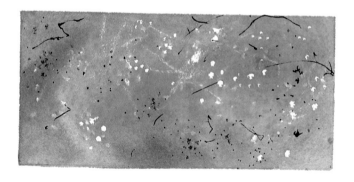

Abram believed what God had said, and the Lord counted his faith as righteousness.

Later God caused him to fall into a very deep sleep, and as he slept he dreamed that his descendants would live as slaves in a strange land, for four hundred years, and that people would treat them cruelly.

But to Abram himself God promised long life and a peaceful end.

In his wanderings with Lot, Abram had become very rich. He had silver and gold and many herds of cattle. Lot, too, had cattle, and sheep, and tents. There was not enough good land to feed everybody, and they started quarreling.

Abram was wise. "Let us have no arguments," he told Lot. "We are members of the same family. Look, we have this whole country to live in. Let us each go our separate ways."

So Lot chose the green plain of the Jordan, and pitched his tents near the city of Sodom, where men were wicked and sinned greatly against God.

Abram lived at Hebron, near the great trees of Mamre, and God promised to give him and his descendants all the land his eyes could see, north and south, and east and west. "Walk the length and breadth of this country," he said. "It is for you."

GOD'S COVENANT WITH ABRAM

Genesis 17

When Abram was a very old man God appeared to him again. The Lord had come to make a very special promise, and when Abram saw him, he fell down and worshiped him.

God said, "Walk in my ways and be free from sin, and you will be the father of many nations. From now on you will be called not Abram but Abraham, which means 'father of many.' My covenant will be everlasting, between me and you, and those who will come after you. I will give you the whole of this land of Canaan, where now you live as a stranger, both to you and to your descendants, forever. And I will be their God.

"As for your wife, Sarai, from now on she will be called Sarah, which means 'princess.' She will have a son and she will be the mother of kings."

Then Abraham laughed to himself. "Can a child be born to a man who is a hundred years old?" he said. "And to a woman who is ninety?"

God said again, "Sarah will have a son, and you will call him Isaac. I will bless him and make him also the father of many. He will be born a year from now." And God left Abraham alone.

GOD DESTROYS THE CITY OF SODOM

Genesis 18–19

God had heard that Sodom, where Lot lived, and its neighbor Gomorrah, were wicked places. He decided to visit them, to see if what men said about them was true. "If it is not, I will know," he said.

"But shall I hide from Abraham what I am going to do? He is my chosen one, and I must keep my promise to him." The problem was that Lot was Abraham's nephew. If God destroyed Sodom, Lot and all his family would perish too.

So God sent two angels as messengers walking toward Sodom. Abraham then approached God, to talk to him.

"Will you destroy good men as well as bad?" he asked. "What if you find fifty good men in Sodom? Are they too to be swept away?"

"If I find fifty good men," God said, "I will spare the city, for their sake."

Then Abraham grew bolder. "What if there are only forty-five good men?" he asked.

"I will spare the city."

"What if there are only forty, or thirty, or even twenty?"

"I will not destroy it for the sake of twenty good men," said God.

Then Abraham, praying that the Lord would not be angry with him, said, "What if you can find only ten good men?"

"I will not destroy it," God promised him.

When the messengers reached Sodom it was evening, and Lot was sitting at the city gates. He greeted them and offered them shelter.

But the two men said, "No. We will spend the night out here, in the square."

Even so, Lot persuaded them to enter his house. But before they had gone to bed they found that it was surrounded. Men had come from all over the city, both young and old, and they demanded that the messengers be brought out to them.

Lot went outside to reason with them. "Do not harm these men," he pleaded. "I have sheltered them in my house."

But the crowd grew angry. "Get out of the way!" they shouted. "You're a stranger here yourself and now you're telling us what to do!" And they tried to break the door down.

But the two messengers pulled Lot back inside the house and barred the door. Then they struck the men outside with blindness so that they could not find their way in.

"Do you have relatives here?" they asked Lot. "Flee from this place. God has commanded us to destroy it."

So Lot went to the men who were going to marry his daughters. "We must all flee from here," he told them. "God is

going to destroy the city." But the young men just laughed at him. They thought he was joking.

When dawn came the two messengers came to Lot and said, "Hurry! Take your wife and your daughters or you will be swept away." But Lot hesitated, so they grasped his hand and the hands of his wife and daughters and led them safely out of Sodom. God had been merciful to them.

When they were outside the city the two men said, "Run for your lives! And do not look back."

But Lot pleaded with them. "I cannot reach the mountains in time," he said. "I will die in the attempt. Let me go to the little town nearby and stay there."

So they promised, and nothing was done until Lot had reached the town of Zoar, in the plains.

By then the sun had risen and God rained down burning sulfur on the wicked cities of Sodom and Gomorrah, destroying all who lived there, and the crops that grew in the fields nearby.

"Do not look back," the messengers had warned Lot. But his wife did look back, and she was turned into a pillar of salt.

ABRAHAM AND ISAAC

Genesis 22

God kept his promise to Abraham and Sarah, and when they were both very old a son was born to them. They named him Isaac. Sarah laughed for joy when she saw her newborn child.

But when Isaac was older, God put his servant Abraham to the test.

"Take your son," God said, "your only son, Isaac, whom you love, and go to the land of Moriah. There I will tell you of a mountain. You must go to it, kill Isaac there, and burn him as a sacrifice to me."

Early the next morning Abraham got up, saddled his donkey, and set off, taking two servants with him, and Isaac, his son. When he had cut wood for the sacrifice he began to look for the mountain. After three days he saw it in the distance.

"Stay here with the donkey," he said to his servants. "The boy and I are going on ahead, to worship the Lord. We will come back to you soon."

As they went along Isaac said, "Father, we have the fire and the wood, but where is the lamb for the burnt offering?"

"God himself will provide the lamb, my son," answered Abraham.

When they reached the mountain Abraham built an altar, piling up wood upon it. Then he bound Isaac with strong cords and laid him on the top.

Finally he picked up his knife, ready to kill his son, but the angel of the Lord called out to him, "Abraham! Abraham!"

"Here I am," he answered.

Then the angel said, "Do not lay a hand upon the lad, and do not harm him in any way. I know now that you fear God because you did not try to save your son, your only son, from me."

Abraham looked up and saw a ram, caught in a thicket by its horns. And instead of his son he sacrificed the ram on the altar. He called the place Jehovah-jireh, "the Lord will provide".

Then the angel spoke to him a second time. "The Lord has sworn this," he said: "'I will bless you, and those that come after you will be like the stars in number, like the grains of sand on the seashore, because you have obeyed my voice.'"

ISAAC AND REBECCA

Genesis 24–25

Sarah, Abraham's wife, had died. He was now a very old man, and the Lord had blessed him in all things. One day he sent for his chief servant and made him swear an oath. "You must swear by the Lord," he said, "that you will not get a wife for my son Isaac from among the Canaanite people with whom we live, but that you will find him one from among my own people. God made me a promise that it was this land he would give to my descendants, so Isaac's wife must come here."

So the servant swore the oath. Then, taking ten of Abraham's camels, and all sorts of treasures from his storehouses, he set off for the town of Nahor. It was near evening when he got there, the time when the women came to draw up water, and he made his camels kneel down at the well.

"O God," he prayed, "give me success today. Perhaps I'll say to one of the women, 'Let down your jar so that I can have a drink,' and she'll say, 'Drink, and let your camels drink too.' Let someone like this be the woman you have chosen for Isaac. It will prove you have shown kindness to his father, Abraham."

While he was praying Rebecca came out carrying an empty water jar on her shoulder. She was young and very beautiful, the daughter of Bethuel, Milcah's son. Abraham was her uncle. Down she went to the well, filled her jar, and pulled it up again.

"Please give me some water from your jar," said Abraham's servant, running to meet her.

"Drink, my lord," she told him, lowering the jar.

Then she said, "I'll draw water for your camels too, so they can drink."

The servant said nothing. He was watching closely, to learn whether God was blessing his journey with success.

When the camels had drunk their fill, he took out a gold earring and two gold bracelets, saying, "Whose daughter are you? Can we spend the night in your house?"

"I am the daughter of Bethuel," she answered. Then she added, "We have plenty of straw and fodder, and room for you to stay with us."

Then the servant worshiped God, saying, "Praise be to the Lord, the God of my master. He has led me here, to the house of Abraham's own family."

Meanwhile Rebecca ran to her mother and told her what had happened. Her brother Laban, seeing the gold ornaments, went to the well and said to Abraham's servant, "Why are you waiting here? The house is ready for you and there is room for your animals too."

The servant explained what had happened, how he had prayed that his journey to find a wife for Isaac would be a success, and how he had seen the beautiful Rebecca coming to the well, how she had been kind to him. "What are you going to do?" he said at last. "Are you going to show kindness to my master and let her be Isaac's wife?"

At that moment Rebecca herself came in. "Take her and go on your way," Laban and Bethuel said. "This is the Lord's doing."

When the servant knew he had been successful he gave thanks to God. Then he brought out gold and jewels and fine clothes for her, and precious gifts for her family too. In the morning they set off for the land of Canaan.

Isaac had gone out into the fields one evening, to pray, and he saw the camels far off. Then he saw Rebecca, and she looked at him. "Who is that man?" she asked the servant.

"He is my master," came the reply, and when she heard this she covered her face with a veil.

Abraham's servant told them all that he had done, and Isaac brought Rebecca into the tent of Sarah, his mother, and made her his wife. He loved her very much.

ESAU AND JACOB

Genesis 25, 27

Isaac was sad because his wife Rebecca had no children. But he prayed to God, and his prayer was answered. When he was sixty years old his wife had twin sons. They were named Esau and Jacob. Esau was very red when he was born, and his skin was covered with hair. Jacob was born holding onto his brother's heel; his name meant "deceiver."

When they grew up the two boys were very different. Esau was a hunter and a countryman; Jacob preferred to stay at home among the tents.

One day Jacob was cooking a stew and

Esau came in, famished after his hunting. "Give me something to eat," he said. "I am dying of hunger."

"First," Jacob told him, "you must sell me your birthright, all that you will inherit from our father as the older son." Esau agreed. "What good is any of it to me?" he said. "I'm going to die of hunger anyway." So he swore an oath to his brother Jacob, that he could have the inheritance. Only when he had done that would Jacob give him food.

Esau thought nothing more about his birthright after this.

When Isaac grew old he became blind. Feeling that his death was near, he sent for Esau, his older son, to give him a special blessing. But before he gave it he asked him to go hunting for the wild game he liked so much.

Rebecca was listening, and as soon as Esau was out of sight she sent for Jacob. "Fetch two goats," she told him, "so that I can prepare a good meal for your father. You can take it to him and pretend to be Esau, and he will give you the blessing before he dies."

"But Esau is hairy," Jacob said, "and my skin is smooth. What if my father touches me? He will know I am tricking him. He will curse me, not bless me."

But Rebecca made him do as she had said. "Let the curse be on me," she told him. She prepared a meal for Isaac, then she dressed Jacob in Esau's best clothes and covered his hands and neck with the goatskins. When the food was ready she gave it to him, and sent him to seek his father's blessing.

"Father," he said to the blind Isaac.

"Who is it?" his father asked.

"It is Esau, your first-born. I have come for your blessing."

The old man asked Jacob to come close. "Let me touch you," he commanded. "It is Jacob's voice," he said to himself, "but the hands are hairy, like Esau's." And he blessed him. Then he ate the food he had brought, drew his son close, and kissed him. As he did so he caught the smell of fine clothes and he said, "The smell of my son is like the smell of a field that the Lord has blessed."

Soon after this Esau came in. He too asked for Isaac's blessing.

"Who are you?" said the blind old man.

"I am Esau, your first-born son," came the answer.

Then Isaac trembled and said, "Who was it then that brought me food and asked for my blessing?"

Esau, knowing he had been deceived, cried out bitterly, "Bless me too, Father!"

But Isaac shook his head. "Your brother has taken away your blessing."

Esau went off, knowing that he must be content with a lesser blessing from his father. But he was determined that one day he would kill his brother.

JACOB'S DREAM

Genesis 28

Rebecca, knowing that Esau had vowed to kill his brother, sent Jacob away, and he set off for Haran, where her family lived. But before he got there he had to stop for the night because the sun had set, so he lay down, using a stone for a pillow.

He dreamed, seeing a great ladder with

its foot resting on the earth and its top reaching to heaven, with angels of God going up and down it.

God himself was standing beside the ladder, and he said to Jacob, "I am the Lord, the God of your fathers, Abraham and Isaac. I will give you and your descendants the land on which you are lying. They will be numberless, like the grains of dust. Through your family all the nations of the earth will be blessed. I am with you, and I will bring you back to this land. Until I have done what I have promised I will not leave you."

When Jacob woke up he thought, "Surely, the Lord is in this place and I never knew." He was afraid now, the place filled him with awe. "This is nothing less than the house of God," he said, "and I have stood at the gate of heaven."

Early next morning he took the stone on which he had rested his head, set it up as a pillar, and poured holy oil upon it.

Then he made a vow. "If God will be with me," he said, "and watch over me on my journey, so that I return in safety to my father's house, then he will be my God too. I will give him a tenth of all I have, and this stone will be his house."

RACHEL AND LEAH

Genesis 29–31

After his dream Jacob traveled on and came at last to Haran, where he met some shepherds. "Do you know Laban, my uncle?" he asked them. "Yes," they said, "and here comes his daughter Rachel. She looks after his sheep."

When Jacob saw Rachel he kissed her and wept, telling her that he was Rebecca's son, and she ran and told her father. Then Laban came out, took Jacob in his arms and led him to their home. "You are my own flesh and blood," he said. Jacob stayed with Laban for a month and worked for him. At the end of the month, Laban asked him what wages he wanted.

Now Laban had two daughters, Leah and Rachel. Rachel was the beautiful one. "I want Rachel to be my wife," Jacob said.

Joseph and the Coat of Many Colors

Genesis 37

Jacob had twelve sons. Reuben was the oldest and Benjamin the youngest. The son Jacob loved best was Joseph, the child who had been born to his wife Rachel after so many years of waiting. To this favorite son he gave a coat of many colors. His brothers were jealous and hated him. In fact, they could not bring themselves to say a kind word to him.

One day Joseph told them about a dream he'd had. "We were in the fields binding sheaves of grain," he said, "and all of a sudden my sheaf stood up while yours gathered around and bowed down to it."

"Are you planning to rule over us then?" his brothers jeered. "Are you planning to be our king?" And they hated him all the more.

Joseph had a second dream. "Listen," he said to his brothers, "in this dream the sun and moon and eleven of the stars were all bowing down to me."

His father, Jacob, was told about this dream too. He was angry with him and said, "Do you mean that your father, mother, and brothers actually bowed down before you?"

"Yes," Joseph replied.

Jacob did not say any more, but he did not forget the strange dream.

The older brothers were sent off to mind their father's flocks near Shechem. Joseph was sent after them, to make sure all was well. For a while he could not find them, but when at last he saw them he noticed they were sitting in a huddle. They were hatching a plot.

"Here comes the dreamer!" one of them said. "Let's kill him and throw his body down one of these old dried-up wells. Then we'll see what happens to his dreams."

But Reuben, the eldest, tried to stop them. "Let's not kill him," he said. "Let's just leave him in a well." His plan was to rescue Joseph and take him home.

So when he arrived they seized him, stripped off his coat of many colors, and threw him down a well. Then they sat down to eat.

While Reuben was away with the flocks, along came some Ishmaelite merchants on camels loaded with spices. They were on their way to Egypt. "There's no point in killing Joseph," one of the brothers said. "After all, he's our own flesh and blood. Let's sell him to these merchants instead."

So they pulled him up out of the well and sold him for twenty pieces of silver.

When Reuben came back he was horrified, but the others took charge, killing a goat and dipping the many-colored coat in it. They went home and showed it

But Joseph was not only brave and true, he was also very handsome, and Potiphar's wife soon fell in love with him. When Joseph would have nothing to do with her she grew angry and told lies about him. He was thrown into prison.

But God was still with Joseph. The jailer trusted him and put him in charge of everything, just as Potiphar had done.

to Jacob. "Is this Joseph's?" they asked.

"It is," cried the old man. "Some wild animal must have torn him to pieces." And he wept bitterly for his favorite son. Nobody could comfort him. "I will go to my grave sorrowing for him," he said.

In the meantime the merchants had reached Egypt and sold Joseph as a slave to Potiphar, the captain of the guard in Pharaoh's palace.

JOSEPH IN POTIPHAR'S HOUSE

Genesis 39–41

Joseph found favor with Potiphar because whatever he did turned out well. Soon he was put in charge of the entire household, and because of Joseph God blessed everyone in it.

In the prison lay the king's baker and the king's cupbearer. One night they both had strange dreams and they asked Joseph to tell them what they meant.

"In my dream," the cupbearer said, "I saw a vine with three branches. All at once it grew grapes. I took the grapes, squeezed them into Pharaoh's cup and put it in his hand."

"The three branches are three days," Joseph told him. "Three days from now you will be restored to your master's favor. Remember me when you are back in his palace. I've done nothing to deserve being thrown into prison."

"I dreamed about three baskets of bread," said the baker. "They were full of pastries for Pharaoh. As I balanced the baskets on my head the birds were eating them."

Joseph's face darkened.

magicians, but no one could tell him what the dreams meant.

It was then that the cupbearer remembered Joseph, and Pharaoh commanded that the young man should be brought before him.

"God will interpret your dreams," Joseph told him, "not me." And then Pharaoh told him about the dreams.

"The three baskets are three days," he told him. "Three days from now Pharaoh will hang you, and the birds will eat your flesh."

The two dreams came true. Within three days the cupbearer was back at the palace, but the poor baker was dead. Joseph stayed locked up in prison. The cupbearer had forgotten all about him.

Some years later Pharaoh himself began to have strange dreams. He was troubled and sent for his wise men and his

In one dream he had seen seven fat cows grazing along the banks of the Nile. Seven thin and scrawny cows came after them and ate them up. But it made no difference. The cows were just as thin as before.

In another dream Pharaoh had seen seven healthy ears of grain growing on a single stalk. Seven withered stalks sprouted beside them, and swallowed them up. "What do my dreams mean?" he asked Joseph.

"Both dreams mean the same thing," Joseph said. "Egypt will have seven years of good harvests, and everyone will have plenty to eat. Then famine will strike the land, and the years of plenty will be forgotten."

Pharaoh listened and knew he needed a wise man to help him. His choice was Joseph, a man on whom God's spirit rested. He was put in charge of everything in the kingdom; only Pharaoh himself was more powerful. And Joseph was wise. During the seven years of plenty he stored up great quantities of grain in the cities. It was like the sand of the sea, too plentiful for him to measure.

But seven years later the famine struck, and the people cried out for food. Joseph opened his storehouses and sold them his grain. People came to him from near and far, for the famine gripped the whole world.

JOSEPH AND HIS BROTHERS

Genesis 42–45

When Jacob heard that there was corn in Egypt he sent ten of his sons to buy some, for there was a famine in Canaan too. He kept Benjamin, the youngest, at his side. He was frightened that something bad would happen to him.

The ten brothers bowed low before Joseph, though they did not realize who he was. He recognized them at once and remembered how they had bowed down before him in his dreams. He decided to test them. "You are spies!" he shouted.

"No," they said. "We have come to buy food. There are ten of us, and another at home. The twelfth is dead."

But Joseph still insisted that they were spies, and he threw them into prison. "You will stay there," he said, "until your youngest brother comes too."

On the third day he told them, "I fear God. Do what I say and you will live." He kept their brother Simeon behind in the prison. The others were set free. "Go and fetch your youngest brother," he told them. "Only then will I believe you are telling me the truth." But even as Simeon was being bound before them, Joseph turned away his face and wept.

Unknown to them, he ordered the money they had paid for their grain to be put back in their sacks. When they found it there, they were afraid. Back at home in Canaan, they told Jacob all that had happened to them at the hands of this strange man who had been so harsh to them.

Jacob was full of grief. "Joseph has gone and Simeon has gone," he said. "Now you want to take Benjamin, too."

When all the food they had brought was gone, they persuaded their father to let them return to Egypt with Benjamin.

They took gifts with them, and twice the money that they needed, to give back what they had found in the sacks and to buy grain.

This time they were taken into Joseph's house. "How is your father?" he asked them. "Alive and well, sir," they told him. "And is this your youngest brother?" he said, looking at Benjamin. "God be gracious to you," he told the boy, and he went away, to weep by himself. Later a great banquet was held for them and they all feasted, but Benjamin's portions were five times bigger than all the others.

As before, Joseph instructed his servants to put the grain money back into his brothers' sacks. Into Benjamin's sack went his special silver cup. Joseph was testing his brothers to see if they really had changed. When they were on their way home, he sent men after them to make them open up the sacks. There in Benjamin's was Joseph's silver cup. He pretended to be very angry now, and he demanded that Benjamin should become his slave.

But his brother Judah pleaded with him. "Our father is old," he said. "If we go back without Benjamin he will die of grief. Let me stay here instead, and let him go back with his brothers."

This was too much for Joseph to bear. He sent everyone away except his brothers, then he told them who he was. He wept so loudly that everybody in the palace heard him.

"I am Joseph," he said, "whom you sold as a slave into Egypt. But be at peace. God has used me to save people's lives. It was he who sent me to Egypt. He had a plan for us." And they threw their arms around one another, and kissed.

Then Joseph told them to return to Canaan, and to bring their families back with them. "Our father must come too," he said, "and you shall all live on the fat of the land."

THE BABY IN
THE BASKET

Exodus 1–2

A new Pharaoh now ruled Egypt. He was very worried about the Israelites in his kingdom. "What if they rise up against me?" he said to himself. "What if they decide to fight on our enemies' side?" So he forced them to work as slaves, making them endure all kinds of hard and bitter labor. Then he devised a cruel plan to get rid of them all.

The plan was this: every baby boy born to an Israelite woman was to be thrown into the River Nile. Nothing could live very long in there.

But one woman, who came from the family of Levi, was determined to save her little son from Pharaoh. The baby was strong and healthy, and for three whole months she managed to keep him hidden.

The time came, however, when she could not hide her precious secret any longer. Someone was bound to find out about the baby sooner or later, and when they did he would be killed. So she wove a little basket out of rushes, made a lid for it, and daubed it all over with clay and tar, to stop the water from coming in. She put the baby inside, and hid the basket in the tall reeds at the edge of the river. Then she crept away. But her daughter Miriam hid in the shadows, just to see what would happen next.

Quite soon Pharaoh's daugher came along for her morning bath, while her maids walked up and down the bank. As she knelt down she saw the little basket hidden in the reeds, and she sent one of her servant girls to bring it out.

When they opened it up they found the baby lying there. He started to cry when he saw all the strange faces. "Why, this is a Hebrew child," the princess said, "one of the Israelites. Poor little thing." She felt sorry for him.

Just then Miriam stepped out of her hiding place. "Shall I find someone to look after the baby?" she cleverly asked. "One of the Hebrew women perhaps?"

And she ran home, and brought her mother back to the little babe, snug in his basket of rushes.

The princess paid the woman wages to look after the child at home, but when he was old enough the princess adopted him and he went to live in the royal palace. She called him Moses because it means "pulled out of the water."

THE BURNING BUSH

Exodus 2–4

Moses was brought up as an Egyptian but he never forgot that he was a Hebrew, one of the children of Israel.

One day, Moses killed an Egyptian for beating one of his people and hid his body in the sand. When Pharaoh heard what he had done he tried to have him killed, but Moses escaped to the land of Midian. He stayed there for many years, married a woman called Zipporah, and had a son called Gershom.

At last the king of Egypt died. But the Israelites still groaned under their slavery and called out to God. He heard them, and remembering his covenant with Abraham and Isaac, he cared about them.

One day Moses was in the desert, tending his father-in-law's sheep on a mountainside. The angel of the Lord appeared to him within flames of fire, in a bush. Moses saw that the bush was on fire and yet was not being burned up, so he went closer. From inside the bush God called out to him, "Moses! Moses!"

"Here I am," he said.

38

God said, "Take off your shoes, for the place you stand on is holy ground." Then he said, "I am the God of Abraham, the God of Isaac, and the God of Jacob." And Moses hid his face; he was afraid to look upon God.

"I have seen the misery of my people in Egypt," God said. "I have heard them cry out, and I have come to rescue them, to take them out of that land into a good land overflowing with milk and honey. You must go to Pharaoh to lead my people out of Egypt."

But Moses said, "Who am I, to be given this task?"

"I will be with you," God promised.

"But what if they ask who has sent me?" pleaded Moses.

God said, "I Am Who I Am. You must say that I Am has sent you. I know that Pharaoh will not let you go, so I will stretch out my hand and strike the Egyptians. After that you will be released."

But Moses was still unsure. "What if they don't believe me?" he said.

Then God made him throw his staff upon the ground, and it turned into a snake. Moses ran away, but God ordered him to pick it up by the tail, and as he did so it became a staff again.

"Take this with you when you go to Pharaoh," God said, "so that you can perform miraculous things with it."

But Moses was still unsure. "Lord, send somebody else," he begged.

Then God told him that his brother Aaron was coming to help him, and that they would go back to Egypt together. "I will teach you what to say," he promised.

THE TEN PLAGUES OF EGYPT

Exodus 7–10

Aaron and Moses went together to Pharaoh, and Aaron threw down the staff at Pharaoh's feet, where it became a snake. But Pharaoh sent for his magicians. They too turned their staffs into snakes. Pharaoh would not listen.

So God spoke to Moses. "When, tomorrow morning, Pharaoh comes to bathe in the Nile, tell him this: 'Let my people go. They are bidden to worship the Lord in the desert.' He will refuse. Then, as a sign that you are speaking for me, raise your staff over the river. It will be turned into blood. So will all the other water in Egypt, the streams, the ponds, everything. It will smell horrible, the fish will die, and there will be nothing to drink. All Egypt will be covered with blood."

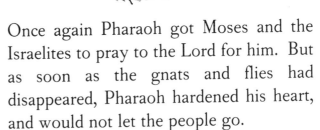

Moses and Aaron obeyed God's command, and the whole land filled with blood. But Pharaoh's magicians did the same thing through their secret skills, and Pharaoh hardened his heart. He would not listen but went into his palace. Meanwhile the Egyptians were digging up the banks of the Nile to find clean water.

Seven days later God sent a plague of frogs upon Egypt. "The Nile will be full of them," he said. "Tell Pharaoh that they will come into his palace and into his bedroom and onto his bed, into the houses of his servants and of his people, into his ovens and into the troughs where they knead their bread." So Aaron stretched his staff over the land of Egypt. And the frogs came, millions of them.

Pharaoh asked Moses to get the Israelites to pray that the frogs would go away. "If you do this I will let the people go," he promised. So God got rid of the frogs. They died, and they were piled up in heaps, so that the kingdom reeked of them. Then Pharaoh changed his mind again.

So God brought a third and a fourth plague upon Egypt. First there was a plague of gnats, then a plague of flies.

Once again Pharaoh got Moses and the Israelites to pray to the Lord for him. But as soon as the gnats and flies had disappeared, Pharaoh hardened his heart, and would not let the people go.

So God sent another plague. This time it killed off all the Egyptian livestock: their horses and their donkeys, their cattle, their sheep, and their goats. None of the animals belonging to the Israelites died, though. God spared them. In spite of this Pharaoh still refused to let the people go.

Next God plagued the Egyptians with horrible boils. Everyone suffered; Pharaoh's own court magicians could not come before their master, they were in such pain. But still he refused to listen to Moses.

So God raised up the worst hailstorms that Egypt had ever known. Cattle left in the fields were killed, and every tree stripped bare. The only place where the terrible hail did not fall was in Goshen, the land of the Israelites.

Pharaoh sent for Moses and Aaron. "This time I will let you go," he said. "The Lord is in the right and I am in the wrong." But as soon as Moses spread out his hands and stopped the storms Pharaoh changed his mind again.

Moses and Aaron went to his palace once more, with a message from the Lord: "Let my people go, or I will bring a plague of locusts upon Egypt."

Pharaoh's servants begged him to release the Israelites. "Egypt is ruined," they told him. "Let these people worship their Lord."

But Pharaoh was suspicious. "Only the men may go," he said. "The women and children must stay behind."

Then Moses stretched his staff over Egypt and brought the locusts. They ate everything the hail had not destroyed; nothing green was left, on the trees or in the fields. Pharaoh was terrified. "I have sinned," he said. "Take away this hideous plague and I will let your people go." But as soon as the locusts had been swept away into the Red Sea he hardened his heart again and said, "No!"

So the Lord told Moses to stretch out his hand toward the sky. "A darkness will spread over Egypt," he said, "a darkness that can be felt." Moses obeyed, and Egypt was in pitch darkness for three days. There was light only in the places where the Israelites lived.

Pharaoh told Moses that the people could go, but he ordered him to leave his flocks and herds behind.

"No," replied Moses. "We must have our animals so that we can make sacrifices to God."

"Out of my sight!" screamed Pharaoh in a fury. "If we ever meet again it will mean death."

"Let it be so," Moses answered. "I will never again appear before you."

THE PASSOVER

Exodus 11–12

God knew that Pharaoh was still going to harden his heart against Moses, so he sent the worst plague of all.

"At about midnight," he said, "I will go throughout Egypt, and all the first-born in the land will die, Pharaoh's son, and the son of the girl who grinds wheat at her mill, even the first-born of the animals themselves. No creature will be spared, and the crying in Egypt will be terrible. But no harm will come to the Israelites. Not so much as a dog will bark at them." God knew that the Egyptians thought highly of Moses. "Ask them to give you silver and gold for your journey," he said.

Then God gave Moses some very special commands. Each Israelite family was to kill a lamb at twilight, and the blood was to be smeared on the doorframes of their house. With the roasted meat they were to eat bitter herbs and bread made without yeast. This was the Lord's Passover, the feast that marked the time when he passed over the houses of the Israelites, and did not harm them. Each year the feast was to be held again, as a reminder.

Moses gathered his leaders together and told them what God had said. "He will see the blood smeared upon your houses," he said, "and he will spare your children."

At midnight the Lord struck down Pharaoh's first-born son, and the first-born of the prisoner in the dungeon, and the first-born of all the cattle. There was a terrible weeping in Egypt then. Not one house was spared.

At last Pharaoh urged the Israelites to be gone. "Go and worship the Lord," he said. "Go, and take your herds with you."

Remembering what God had told them, they took silver and gold from the Egyptians. They left in such a hurry that there was no time to add yeast to the dough in their kneading troughs.

There were about six hundred thousand men, and women and children too, and great flocks and herds which they drove ahead of them. They had been slaves in Egypt for over four hundred years. Now they were free.

THE WALLS OF WATER

Exodus 13–15

The Israelites traveled across the desert toward the Red Sea, and God guided them. By day he went before them in a pillar of cloud, to hide them, and by night in a pillar of fire, to give them light.

The minute Pharaoh heard that they had fled from his kingdom he went after them. He took six hundred of his best chariots, set off across the desert with his horsemen and his troops, and overtook them by the sea near Pi Hahiroth.

The Israelites were terrified when they saw a great army sweeping down on them, and they cried to Moses, "Did you bring us to this desert to die because there were no graves in Egypt? We'd be better off serving the Egyptians."

But Moses told them not to be afraid. "Stand firm," he said. "The Lord will fight for you. You will never see these Egyptians again."

Then God said to Moses, "Lift your staff and stretch out your hand over the sea to divide the waters, so that the Israelites can go across the sea on dry land."

And his angel, who had been traveling at the front, came behind. So did the pillars of cloud and of fire. When night came they stood between the two armies, bringing light to one and darkness to the other.

Moses stretched out his hand over the sea, and a great wind blew up, revealing dry land, and the Israelites crossed over in safety with huge walls of water towering up on their right and their left.

The Egyptians went after them, into the sea. But toward morning God looked down from the pillars of fire and cloud and threw them into confusion. Chariot wheels were torn off, horses perished, and the Egyptians cried out, "Let us get away! The Lord is on their side!"

God commanded Moses to stretch out his hand a second time, and when day came, the sea swept back to its place, drowning the entire Egyptian army. Not one man survived.

Then sang Moses and the children of Israel this song:

I will sing unto the Lord, for he hath triumphed gloriously: the horse and his rider hath he thrown into the sea.

The Lord is my strength and song, and he is become my salvation: he is my God.

44

CROSSING THE DESERT

Exodus 15–17

The Israelites had escaped from the Egyptians, but they were unhappy, wandering in a vast desert. They were hungry and homeless. For three days after leaving the Red Sea they were without water. When at last they found some, at Marah, it was too bitter to drink. They began to grumble.

Moses cried out to the Lord, and God showed him a piece of wood, which he threw into the water, making it sweet to drink. "If you listen to my voice," God told the Israelites, "if you keep my laws and do what is good, I will not punish you with plagues as I did the Egyptians."

And when they reached Elim they found seventy palm trees there, and twelve springs of water.

But soon the Israelites grew discontented. "If only we had died in Egypt!" they said. "At least we had plenty to eat there. Here in this wilderness we are starving to death."

Then God promised Moses that he would provide food for them for six days each week, that bread would come down from heaven like rain. They were to gather just enough each day, but on the sixth day they were to gather twice as much as they needed so that they could rest on the seventh day.

And God appeared to them all in a cloud of glory. "At twilight you will eat meat," he said, "and in the morning you will eat bread. By this you will know that I am the Lord your God."

That night little birds called quail, which were good to eat, covered the camp, and in the morning the Israelites saw that a dew had fallen. When it had melted, thin flakes like frost were left in its place. "What is this?" they asked.

"It is the bread which the Lord has sent for you," Moses told them.

The bread was called manna. It was white like coriander seed and it tasted of wafers made with honey. Each day the people gathered it up. But sometimes they were greedy, disobeying God by keeping some till the next morning. That bread went bad, and was full of maggots.

On the seventh day some of them went out to get more, instead of gathering double the day before and resting on the Sabbath as God had commanded. He was angry with them. "How long will you refuse to obey me?" he said. But he still looked after them, and the Israelites ate manna for forty years, until the time they reached Canaan.

In spite of God's goodness the Israelites remained ungrateful, and when the water ran out again they were angry with Moses.

"What am I to do with these people?" Moses cried in despair. "They seem ready to stone me to death."

"Walk on ahead," God told him. "Take some of your elders with you and the staff with which you struck the waters of the Nile. Go to Horeb and strike the rock with it. Water will come gushing forth." So Moses did what God had said, and the people drank their fill.

THE TEN COMMANDMENTS

Exodus 19–20, 32–34, Psalm 91

Three months to the day after the Israelites had left Egypt they camped in front of Mount Sinai.

Moses went before God to speak to him, and God reminded him of all he had done for the children of Israel. "I have carried you on eagles' wings," he told him, "and brought you to myself. If you will obey me," he said, "you will be special to me. You will be a kingdom of priests, a holy nation.

"Now tell the people to prepare themselves. Let them wash their clothes and be ready for me. On the third day I will come down upon Mount Sinai. But they must not set foot upon the mountain."

On the third day a thick cloud hung over Mount Sinai. There was thunder and lightning, and the sound of a trumpet growing louder and louder.

Moses spoke, and the voice of God answered him. These are the words he carried back to the people:

I AM THE LORD YOUR GOD, WHO BROUGHT YOU OUT OF EGYPT.

You shall have no other gods before me.

You shall not make idols and worship them.

You shall not misuse the name of the Lord your God.

Remember the sabbath day by keeping it holy. You shall work for six days, but the seventh is the sabbath of the Lord your God.

Honor your father and your mother.

You shall not murder.

You shall not commit adultery.

You shall not steal.

You shall not tell lies against your neighbor.

You shall not covet the things that belong to your neighbor.

These were the Ten Commandments.

At the thunder and the lightning and the sight of Mount Sinai wreathed in smoke, the people trembled, and they stayed far off.

But Moses went close to the thick darkness where God was, and God talked with him, explaining all the laws by which the children of Israel should be governed, and what his commandments meant. Moses was alone with God for forty day and forty nights.

God had told the Israelites not to worship other gods but they paid no attention. They had grown tired of waiting for Moses to come down from the mountain, and they gathered around Aaron, asking him to make gods for them.

Aaron told them all to remove their earrings, and with the gold he made an idol shaped like a calf. They worshiped it, sacrificed before it, and then sat down to eat and drink their fill.

God was very angry. "These people are stiff-necked and obstinate," he said to Moses. But Moses begged God to be merciful, and he came down from Mount Sinai with the two tablets of stone on which God's commandments were written.

When Moses saw the golden calf, however, and the people dancing, he broke the tablets into pieces and burned the golden idol in the fire.

God struck the people with a plague for what they had done, sparing only those who had remained faithful to him. The Israelites were sorry now. They took off all their gold and jewels and waited to see what the Lord would do.

Moses pleaded with God for them, and God made this promise: "My Presence will go with you and I will give you rest." Then Moses said to God, "Show me your glory," and God answered, "I will put you in the cleft of a rock when my glory passes by, and I will cover you with my hand. Then I will take away my hand and you will see only my back. For no one may see my face and live."

So Moses saw the glory of the Lord, and afterward his face shone like the sun.

This is a psalm, a song of praise. It praises God for the love and protection he gives to those who, like Moses, put their trust in him:

He that dwelleth in the secret place of the Most High shall abide under the shadow of the Almighty.

I will say unto the Lord, he is my refuge and my fortress, my God; in him will I trust.

Surely he shall deliver thee from the snare of the fowler, and from the noisome pestilence.

He shall cover thee with his feathers, and under his wings shalt thou trust: his truth shall be thy shield and buckler.

Thou shalt not be afraid for the arrow that flieth by day;

Nor for the pestilence that walketh in darkness; nor for the destruction that wasteth at noonday . . .

There shall no evil befall thee, neither shall any plague come near thy dwelling.

For he shall give his angels charge over thee, to keep thee in all thy ways.

They shall bear thee up in their hands, lest thou dash thy foot against a stone.

Thou shalt tread upon the lion and adder: the young lion and the dragon shalt thou trample under feet.

Because he hath set his love upon me, therefore will I deliver him; I will set him on high, because he hath known my name.

He shall call upon me, and I will answer him: I will be with him in trouble; I will deliver him, and honor him.

With long life will I satisfy him, and show him my salvation.

THE ARK AND THE TABERNACLE

Exodus 25–40

Moses was on Mount Sinai for forty days and forty nights, talking with God, and it was then that God told him exactly how he wanted the children of Israel to worship him.

First they were to bring him gifts, the best they had: gold, silver, and bronze; fine linen, sheepskins, and leather; acacia wood and olive oil to burn in the lamps; and precious jewels to put on their priestly robes. He wanted the people to build a tabernacle, a holy tent for the worship of their Lord, and he gave them careful plans, telling them precisely how to do it.

To contain the tablets on which his laws were written, the people were to make a special box called an ark. It was to be fashioned from acacia wood and covered with gold, and two gold cherubim were to sit on it. There was to be a table,

also covered with gold, and the dishes and plates for this were to be made out of gold too. He commanded them to make a great candlestick for seven candles, branching up like a tree, with its cups like almond flowers.

The holy tent was to be covered with curtains made of goat's hair, and on top the people were to lay sheepskins dyed red. Inside, curtains were to separate off two Holy Places. Into one, the Most Holy Place, they must put the ark that contained the laws of God. Everything was to be done by the most skilled craftsmen of the nation—goldsmiths and workers in wood, weavers and dyers—for these things were all to honor God himself.

Aaron and his four sons were chosen as priests to serve God in his tabernacle, and for them God commanded that special robes should be worn, rich robes of the finest linen decorated with gold and precious stones. Aaron himself was to wear a turban with a gold engraving upon it saying, "Holy to the Lord." This was to remind him always that, whatever bad things the children of Israel might do, their sacrifices would be accepted by God.

Before Moses came down from the mountain the Lord told him again that the seventh day, the Sabbath, was to be kept holy. In this way the Israelites would remember how God rested from his labors on the seventh day. The Sabbath was to be a sign between him and his chosen people, forever and ever.

MOSES AND AARON DIE

Deuteronomy 34, Numbers 20, 27

All this time the Israelites were steadily traveling north. God had promised that Moses would lead them to the good land of Canaan, the land overflowing with milk and honey. The tabernacle went with them on their journey, and the Lord was always with them.

Moses did not live to enter the land of Canaan, though God showed it to him, from the top of Mount Pisgah. "I have let you see it," the Lord said, "but you will not cross over into it." Moses was a very old man, but he was still strong, and his eyes good enough to see the Promised Land. He died in Moab, and the Israelites grieved for him. No one who ever came after had done such wonders, or had fought for them against Pharaoh, or had known God face to face.

Aaron, his brother, who had always been at his side, had also died. So the children of Israel were given a new leader. This was an answer to Moses' prayer for the people, that they would not wander about without a leader and be like sheep that had no shepherd. The man God provided for them was Joshua the son of Nun.

(Here, the five books of scripture that the Jewish people call the Torah come to an end.)

Joshua Leads the People

Joshua 1–4

God made a promise to Joshua: "As I was with Moses, so I shall be with you. I shall never leave you. Be strong, and very courageous, for the Lord your God will be with you wherever you go."

Then Joshua prepared his people to cross the River Jordan. On the other side lay the land of Canaan, the land God had promised to them. But first there were many dangers to be faced, so Joshua sent out two spies to the city of Jericho, to see what was happening.

The king heard about it and sent a message to a woman named Rahab, because the spies had been seen entering her house. "Bring the men out!" he ordered. But the woman had hidden them, under some stalks of flax she'd laid out to dry on her roof. "They left at dusk," she told the king's servants. "If you hurry you may catch up with them."

At nightfall she crept up to the roof and talked to the two spies. "We know that God has given your people this land," she said, "and we are all terrified about what might happen to us when you invade it. I have been kind to you. In return, will you be kind to me, and spare my family? Don't let us be put to death."

"Very well. We shall spare your life if you will spare ours," the men promised. "Don't give us away, and we'll treat you kindly when the Lord gives us this land."

Now the woman's house was set into the city wall, and she let them down on a rope, so they escaped. "Flee to the hills," she told them. "Hide there for three days."

The men gave her a scarlet cord and told her to tie it in the window through which they had escaped, and to bring all her relatives inside the house. "No one must leave," they said. "If they do we cannot be blamed if they are killed."

So the woman agreed and tied the scarlet cord in her window. Meanwhile the spies went back to Joshua and told him all that had happened. "The Lord has given the whole land to us," they said. "The people are fainting away, for fear of what might happen."

For three days the Israelites camped by the River Jordan. "Prepare yourselves," Joshua told them. "God is going to do amazing things for you."

And God did. The ark, the special box containing his laws, was carried ahead of the people by the priests, and as soon as they set foot in the river the waters stopped flowing, heaping themselves up to reveal dry land. Then all the people crossed over safely. After them came a great army of forty thousand men, all armed for battle.

Joshua ordered twelve men to take stones on their shoulders and mark the place where the waters of the Jordan had been cut off. The stones were a reminder of the twelve tribes of Israel, and of how God had kept his word. They were set up at Gilgal and Joshua said to the Israelites, "When your children ask what these stones are for, this is what you must tell them: the Lord our God dried up the Jordan, just as he dried up the waters of the Red Sea, so that all the earth might know the hand of the Lord is powerful, and that we must fear him."

THE FALL OF JERICHO

Joshua 5–6

Joshua approached Jericho, and as he got near he saw a man with a sword in his hand. "Are you on our side or on the side of our enemies?" Joshua asked.

"I am neither. I command the army of the Lord," was the reply. "Take off your shoes. The place you are standing on is holy." Then Joshua knew that God was there, and he unlaced his sandals.

Because the Israelite army was so close, the city of Jericho was all barricaded up. Not a crack showed in its great walls. No one went in or out.

God spoke to Joshua. "Jericho is yours," he said, "so are its king and its army, if you will follow these commands. First, the army must march right around the city walls, and before them must march seven priests, carrying my ark, blowing rams' horns. This must be done for six days. On the seventh day they must march around the walls seven times, and all the while the priests must blow their horns. When they hear the noise all the people must shout aloud. The walls of the city will fall down, and Jericho will easily be taken. You will be able to walk straight into it."

Joshua told the people exactly what God had said. But he also gave them a warning. "Be silent," he told them. "There must be no battle cries, no shouting. Do not say a word until I give you the signal."

All was done as the Lord had commanded. The army and the priests marched round and round the city, carrying the ark before them. When, on the seventh day, the last march was completed, Joshua cried to the people,

"Shout! The Lord has given you the city! Jericho now belongs to him. No one will be spared except Rahab and her family, because she hid our spies. Go in, but do not take any gold or silver. It is all to go into the Lord's treasury. If you steal it, you yourselves will be destroyed."

Then the great trumpets sounded, and the walls of Jericho came tumbling down. In charged the Israelites, and with their swords they destroyed every living thing they saw: men and women, young and old, cattle, sheep, and donkeys.

Joshua sent his spies to Rahab's house. They guided her and her family to safety, and she lived as an Israelite from that day forward.

Jericho was never to be rebuilt. "He who rebuilds it will be cursed," said Joshua.

The Lord had truly been at his side that day, and his fame spread far and wide.

GIDEON

Judges 6–7

The Israelites were not always faithful to their Lord. Sometimes they turned away from him and worshiped other gods. To show he was angry with them God let them fall into the hands of the Midianite people for seven long years. These men were cruel. They came down like locusts, destroying the Israelites' crops and their livestock. The Israelites had to hide in caves and in the clefts of the mountains.

Then a good man came to save them. He was very young, and his name was Gideon. One day an angel had appeared to him as he sat under an oak tree. "The Lord is with you, mighty warrior," the angel said.

Gideon did not understand. "Sir," he replied, "if God is really with us, why are we suffering so? He has abandoned us to the Midianites."

Then the Lord himself spoke to Gideon. "Go in the strength you have," he said, "and save Israel."

Gideon was afraid. "How can I?" he said. "My tribe is weak and I myself am just a nobody," and he asked for a sign that it really was God who had spoken.

He was told to prepare food and drink and put them on a rock. The angel of God touched them with his staff, a fire blazed up, and they burned away to nothing.

Then the angel vanished. "I have seen the Lord's angel face to face," said Gideon.

But he was still not quite sure that God really wanted him to save Israel, and he asked for more proof. One night he put some wool on the ground and asked God to wet it with dew but to keep the ground dry. In the morning he wrung a whole bowlful of water from the wool, but the ground all around it was as dry as a bone. The next night the opposite happened. A dew fell and wet the ground, but the fleece itself remained dry. By these signs and wonders Gideon knew that God was really with him.

He took a great army of men and camped at the spring of Harod, south of the Midianite camp. But God told him his

army was too big. "Israel must not boast that she has saved herself," he said. "Tell the people that anyone who trembles with fear need not fight." That day twenty-two thousand men went away, leaving only ten thousand.

But God said there were still too many, and he told Gideon to take them all to the waterside. Everyone was thirsty and drank. Some lapped up the water like dogs, others scooped it up with their hands.

God was watching. "Three hundred men scooped up the water putting their hands to their mouths," he said. "With them I will save Israel." So the rest of the great army was sent away.

At night Gideon crept over to the enemy's camp. He knew the Midianites were powerful; there were thousands of them, and their camels were too many to count, like grains of sand. He kept very still, and listened to what they were talking about.

One man said, "I dreamed last night that a round barley loaf came tumbling into the Midianite camp. It hit a tent and the tent collapsed!"

His friend interpreted the dream. "The loaf is the sword of Gideon," he said. "This whole camp will fall to him. God will give him the victory."

And God did. Each of his three hundred men was given a trumpet, and an empty jar with a flaming torch inside. "Follow me and watch carefully," Gideon told them. "When we blow our trumpets, blow yours and shout, 'For the Lord and for Gideon!'"

At his signal the men smashed their jars, held up the trumpets and the torches, and gave the great victory cry. The Midianites were confused and terrified. Some fled away, but Gideon's men went after them and brought back the heads of two enemy leaders, as he waited for them by the River Jordan.

SAMSON

Judges 13–16

Once again the Israelites were intent on doing evil. This time God delivered them up to the Philistines, and they suffered hardship under them for forty years.

But the Lord had not deserted them, and he raised up a man called Samson, who was born to a woman with no children. She had been barren all her life.

Before he was born an angel appeared to his mother. "Do not cut his hair," he said; "this will show he is very special. Your son will be a Nazirite, set apart to serve God. Through him the Lord will begin to deliver your people from the Philistines." When the child was born, God blessed him, and his Spirit began to stir in him.

When Samson grew up he fell in love with a Philistine woman. As he journeyed to meet her, a young lion came roaring toward him. Samson tore it apart with his bare hands, as easily as he might have torn a young goat.

Some time later Samson went back to marry the Philistine woman and, when he passed the place where he had killed the lion, he found that bees had swarmed inside its carcass. He scooped out the honey and ate it as he traveled along.

At his wedding there were thirty guests, and he set them a riddle:

"Out of the eater came something to eat.
Out of the strong flowed something
    sweet."

It was about the lion and the honeybees. They were desperate to find the answer, because their reward for guessing correctly was to be thirty sets of fine clothes. But no one could solve the riddle, and they got angrier and angrier. In the end they threatened to burn down the bride's house with her family in it if she didn't pry the answer out of Samson and tell them.

His wife begged him so hard he gave in and explained the riddle. But he was angry too, for he knew she had been unfaithful to him and given away the answer. He went down to Ashkelon and killed thirty Philistines in his rage, gave their clothes to his guests, then handed over his wife to one of them.

Samson was still angry at being so cheated. So he caught three hundred foxes, tied blazing torches to their tails, and sent them running into the Philistines' wheatfields. The wheat was destroyed, together with their vineyards and their olive groves.

In revenge the Philistines burned his bride to death. Samson went mad then, killing those who had wronged him. There seemed no end to his fury. He was possessed of the most colossal strength, a strength that could come only from God.

In fear his own people bound him

securely. They planned to hand him over to the Philistines to make up for the terrible things he had done. But he burst his bonds, grabbed the jawbone of a donkey, and killed a thousand men with it. After that no one dared stand in his way.

When Samson fell in love with a woman named Delilah his enemies thought their best chance had come. "See if you can get Samson to tell you the secret of his strength," they told her. "In return we will each give you eleven hundred shekels of silver." So greedy Delilah asked him where his strength came from. "If I am tied up with seven new leather thongs it will leave me," he told her. But when he was tied up and the Philistines burst in on him he snapped the thongs as if they were bits of burnt string.

Then he said new ropes would sap him of his strength. But the minute Delilah shouted a warning he snapped them like threads.

Then he told her to braid his hair and attach it to her weaving loom, and he fell asleep. But when she woke him he merely dragged the loom across the room. He still hadn't told her his secret.

"You don't love me," she wheedled. "You keep making a fool of me." For days and days she nagged him until at last he told her the truth.

"My head has never been shaved," he said. "If my hair is cut I will be as weak as any other man." And he fell asleep.

The Philistines brought Delilah the silver they had promised, and in return she got a man to shave off all his hair. Now that he had no strength to resist they seized him easily, gouged out his eyes, and threw him in prison. He became a laughingstock, and one day they dragged

him out of prison to make him do tricks for them. "Entertain us, Samson!" they roared to the great blind man.

"Put me where I can feel the pillars of the temple," he said. It was full; everyone had turned out to laugh at Samson. They did not hear him praying to the Lord, "Give me strength one last time, so that I can get revenge for my two eyes." But God heard him.

"Let me die with the Philistines!" Samson cried. Leaning against the huge pillars that held the temple up, he pushed with all his strength, bringing it crashing down on all who were inside. In death Samson killed far more people than he had in life.

RUTH

Ruth

Long ago there was a great famine in the land of Judah. A man named Elimelech, with his wife Naomi and their two sons, went to find food in a foreign country called Moab. While they were living there Elimelech died. Both the sons found wives for themselves. One was called Orpah and the other Ruth.

They lived in Moab for ten years, but then both the sons died too, and old Naomi, left all alone, decided to go back to her own country of Judah. She had heard that God had blessed it with food again.

But she told Ruth and Orpah to go back to their own families. "You have been good to me," she said. "Now may God be good to you. May he bring you new husbands, and new homes." And she kissed them.

Ruth and Orpah wept bitterly. "Do not send us away," they pleaded. But Naomi was firm. "Go back to your own people," she said, "for I am an old woman now. I have no sons left to be your husbands."

So, very sadly, Orpah said goodbye, but Ruth clung to Naomi. "Do not ask me to leave you," she said, "for where you go I will go too, and where you stay I will stay. Your people shall be my people, and your God my God. Nothing but death will part us now."

So Ruth and Naomi traveled on together until they reached Bethlehem, just as the harvest was beginning. Ruth went into the fields to follow the reapers, hoping to pick up a few ears of grain that had been left behind.

Now all the surrounding lands belonged to a very rich man named Boaz. He noticed the foreign girl gathering grain in his field, and he asked his reapers who she was. "She came from Moab," they told him, "with old Naomi. She's been here since daybreak, following us around and picking up the stray ears of grain."

Then Boaz called Ruth over to him and told her to stay close to his servants. "If you're thirsty," he said, "drink some of the water they have brought."

"But why are you so kind to me?" she said in amazement. "I'm just a foreigner."

"I have heard how good you have been to Naomi," he told her, "how you left your own home to be with her, and came instead to a strange land. May the Lord reward you, Ruth, for what you have

done, the Lord God of Israel under whose wings you have taken refuge."

When the reapers stopped to eat, he made sure she had food too. "Don't scold her," he whispered to them, "but let her go among the barley sheaves and gather grain. In fact, drop some in her path deliberately, so she has plenty."

When she got home again, Ruth told Naomi all about Boaz and his kindness. "Blessings on him," said the old woman thankfully. "This shows that God still remembers us and cares for us, even now, when all our loved ones are dead." Then she told Ruth to tell Boaz that he was a relative of Elimelech, her dead husband. "Perhaps he will give us more help," she said.

So Ruth went off to find him, and when he heard what Naomi had said he told her to hold her cloak out wide. Into it he poured a great measure of barley, and she put it on her back and went home to show Naomi. "I believe that Boaz will not rest

until he has done even more for us," the old woman told her.

And she was right, because Boaz sent for Ruth, and asked her to be his wife. In time she bore him a son. "Blessed be the Lord today," Naomi's friends told her joyfully. "He did not leave you alone. This grandson has come in your old age. And your daughter-in-law, who loves you so dearly, has done more for you in the end than all your sons!" Then Naomi took her little grandson, and held him very close.

The neighboring women called the baby Obed, and he became the father of Jesse, who in turn became the father of King David.

GOD CALLS SAMUEL

1 Samuel 1–3

There was once a woman named Hannah who had no children. One day she went into the temple at Shiloh and prayed that God would be merciful to her and give her child. As she prayed, she wept.

Eli, the priest, heard her make a promise to the Lord. "If you will grant me a son," she said, "I will give him to you, and he will serve you."

"Go in peace," Eli told her, "and may God grant you what you have asked."

Quite soon Hannah gave birth to a son. Like Samson's, his hair was not cut short. He too was a Nazirite, set apart to serve God. She named him Samuel, which means "the gift." When he was still very young she took him to the house of the Lord. There was Eli, who had heard her prayers and her crying. "I prayed for this child," she told him. "Now I am giving him to the Lord." And she left him there.

Before she went away she prayed:

"There is no one holy like the Lord . . . there is no rock like our God."

Eli's sons served in the temple, but they were wicked men. They did not honor the Lord or his sacrifices. Eli pleaded with them, but they would not listen to him. Not even when a man of God came and made a terrible prophecy to them. "God will cut this family off," he said. "No one will live to be old. Those who survive will be blinded with tears, and their children will die in the prime of life. In your place God will raise up a faithful priest, who will do his will."

Those were sad days in the temple of Shiloh. No one was granted visions any more. But one night, as Samuel lay asleep near the ark, he heard a voice calling. "Samuel," it said.

"Here I am," the boy answered, and he ran to Eli who was lying in his usual place. The lamp of the Lord was still burning, the great gold candlestick whose light must never go out before morning.

"I did not call you, my son," Eli said. "Go back to sleep."

So Samuel lay down, but the voice came again, and then a third time. "Samuel," it said.

"I did not call you, child," Eli told him. He knew now that it was God's voice. "Next time you hear it, say, 'Speak, Lord, for your servant is listening.'"

The boy did as he was told, and this time God spoke to him, and explained how the wicked sons of Eli would not live to serve him.

In the morning Samuel was afraid to tell the old priest what he had heard, but Eli persuaded him, and in the end he told the whole story.

"He is the Lord; let him do what is good in his eyes," said Eli.

So as Samuel grew up the Lord was with him, and he was recognized by the people as a prophet of the Lord.

SAUL BECOMES KING

1 Samuel 8–10

Samuel ruled over Israel all his life, as judge, and when he grew old he appointed his sons to rule in his place. But they were no better than the sons of Eli; they were dishonest and let people bribe them.

The people were weary of them. "Your sons do not follow your good example," they said, "and you are an old man now. We want a king to rule over us, like other nations. Give us a king."

Samuel was unhappy when he heard this, and he turned to God for help. The Lord explained that it was not Samuel they were rejecting, but God himself. "You must give them a solemn warning," he said, "that a king may not turn out as they might wish."

So Samuel went back to the people and told them that a king would treat them harshly, making their sons and daughters work hard for him, in his armies and his fields and his kitchens, taking the crops they had raised for his own use and giving them to his favorites, making them all his slaves.

But the people of Israel would not listen. "Give us a king!" they cried.

So they got their king, a man named Saul, and this is how it came about. His father, Kish, sent him out one day with a servant to hunt for some missing donkeys. They searched high and low but could not find them, ending up in a place called Zuph, where Samuel had come to make a special sacrifice. He was on his way up to a high place, to make his offering to God on the altar there.

When he saw Saul, Samuel knew that the tall young man was the king whom God had sent. He told him to go ahead of him, up the hill, and that in the morning he would tell him all that was in his own heart. "Do not worry about the donkeys," he said. "They have been found. This message is far more important, that the desire of all Israel is turned to you. You are the people's hope."

Saul ate with Samuel and received a choice piece of meat that had been laid aside for him, and that night they talked about Saul, and how he was to be made king. At daybreak Samuel anointed him with oil, then he sent him on his way.

When Saul met his family again he told them nothing about it, only that the missing donkeys had been found.

Meanwhile Samuel had called together the Israelites at a place called Mizpah, reminding them how they had demanded that God give them a king. Out of all the tribes, that of Benjamin, the very smallest, was chosen, and out of this tribe was chosen Saul, son of Kish. But no one could find him. He had run away and hidden in the baggage.

At last they brought him into the open. He was taller by a head than any other man. "Do you see whom the Lord has chosen?" Samuel said. "There is nobody else like him."

And all the people shouted, "Long live the king!"

GOD CALLS DAVID

1 Samuel 15–16

Saul was a warlike king, forever fighting against the Philistines and greedily plundering their goods, in spite of God's commands. What Samuel had told the people came true, and in the end the Lord rejected him.

Saul had been fighting against the Amalekites, and Samuel had given him God's orders about what to do. He was to destroy the people and all that they owned, their sheep, their cattle, and their donkeys. Nothing at all was to be left.

But Saul disobeyed. He indeed conquered the Amalekites but he destroyed only what was weak and useless. The best of the cattle, anything plump and fat, he kept for himself and his men.

God saw what he had done, and he spoke to Samuel. "I am grieved that I ever made Saul king," he said. "He has turned away his face from me." In his sorrow Samuel cried all night to the Lord.

In the morning he went to find Saul, but the king had gone to Carmel, to set up a monument to himself. When they met at last, the old man said, "What is this bleating and mooing I can hear?"

"We kept back the best of the enemy's beasts to sacrifice to the Lord," Saul told him.

Then Samuel reminded him of how God had plucked him from the smallest tribe of all, to make him king, and of how he had commanded him to wipe out the Amalekites completely. "Why did you plunder and disobey?" he said.

Saul tried to defend himself. "I have brought back Agag their king," he boasted.

But Samuel said:

"Does the Lord delight in burnt offerings and sacrifices
as much as in obeying the voice of the Lord? . . .
Because you have rejected the word of the Lord,
he has rejected you as king."

Saul begged forgiveness. "I have sinned," he said. But Samuel turned away from him. As he did so Saul caught hold of his robe and tore it. "Today," Samuel told him, "the Lord has torn away from you the kingdom of Israel and has given it to someone better."

The old man never saw Saul again, though he mourned for him.

God sent Samuel to Jesse, in Bethlehem. It was one of this man's sons who was to become king in Saul's place. At first he was sure the Lord's chosen one was a tall youth called Eliab, but God said no, and that Samuel was to pay no heed to anyone's appearance. "The Lord does not look upon the things man looks at," he said. "The Lord looks at the heart."

Seven of Jesse's sons were brought before Samuel, but none was God's chosen one. At last the youngest was sent for: David, who had been out tending his father's sheep. "He is the one," God told Samuel, and the old man anointed him there, in the presence of his brothers.

The Lord's Spirit had left Saul now, and he was in torment. His servants said, "Let us find someone to play on the harp to you. You will feel better then."

Someone told him about David: "He can play the harp, he is brave, and the Lord is with him."

So they sent messengers to Jesse, and David came to Saul's court. The king liked him and made him his armor bearer, and whenever evil thoughts troubled the king, the music of David's harp made him feel better.

DAVID AND GOLIATH

1 Samuel 17

Now King Saul and his Israelites had been fighting for many years against the Philistines and once more the two armies were facing each other, this time across a deep valley. From the Philistines' camp strode a huge man named Goliath. He wore a massive bronze helmet and a clanking coat of thick chain mail, and his great spear was as thick as a tree trunk.

"Send a man out to fight me!" he bellowed. "If I kill him, you will all become our slaves!" At the sound of his voice the Israelites quaked in terror; no one dared move an inch.

Morning and evening, for forty days, Goliath came and jeered at the terrified soldiers. David, who was up in the mountains looking after his father's sheep, heard about it and secretly wondered what to do. Then his father, Jesse, gave him some food to take to his brothers, who were soldiers in Saul's army. While he was talking to them Goliath appeared before them yet again.

"Come and fight!" he yelled. The Israelites all ran away, but David knew that God was on their side, and he told the king that he would fight the giant himself.

"No!" Saul said in dismay. "He is a great warrior and you are a mere boy."

But David answered, "The God who saved me from the lion and the bear that attacked my sheep will surely save me from Goliath." When he heard this the king said, "Go, and may the Lord be with you," and he gave David armor, a coat of mail, a helmet, and a sword.

Everything was so heavy that the boy could hardly walk, so he took it all off. Instead he picked up five smooth pebbles from the bed of the stream. Then he set off with his little leather sling to meet the giant. Goliath sneered at him. "I'll soon finish you off!" he yelled. "Then I'll feed your body to the crows."

But David replied, "You may have a spear and a javelin but I have the power of Almighty God. It is you who will die today."

As the giant rushed upon him, David took one of the pebbles and fired it straight at Goliath's forehead. It sank deep into the flesh, and the huge man rolled dead at David's feet.

And from that day on, David no longer lived in the royal palace as a servant but as a trusted friend. His dearest friend there was Jonathan, the king's son. And Jonathan loved David as he loved his own soul.

SAUL IS JEALOUS

1 Samuel 18–31, 2 Samuel 1

Saul grew jealous of David and of his friendship with Jonathan. He was jealous of his great strength, too. When David killed Goliath and triumphed over the Philistines the Israelite women sang this song:

Saul has slain his thousands
and David his tens of thousands.

Saul hated this. "He will want my throne soon," he said, and the next day he tried to kill David by pinning him to the wall with his spear, but David escaped.

Then the king tried to trap him another way. He offered David his daughter Michal as a bride, but in payment he was to kill a hundred Philistines. Off to battle went David, and came back with two hundred dead Philistines to claim his bride. From that day on Saul was even more afraid of David. Ever afterward the jealous king was his enemy.

Jonathan, the king's son, was David's dearest friend, and he pleaded with his father not to have David killed. "He risked his life against the Philistines," he told him. "Why kill an innocent man?" For a while Saul softened toward David, but then his jealousy broke out again. He tried to have him murdered in his bed, but David's wife found out, and they put an idol there instead, while David escaped through the window.

Jonathan knew how anxious his father was to get rid of David, but he was determined never to desert his friend.

One day the king decided to hold a great feast, but David stayed in hiding and Saul was furious at his absence. Now Jonathan had already promised to give David a secret sign. In the field where David hid, Jonathan would shoot three arrows and send a little boy to pick them up. If he told the boy the arrows had fallen far away it meant that David was to flee from the palace and never trust Saul again. Because Saul was so angry, this is what happened, and David and Jonathan had to say goodbye. They kissed each other, and wept.

Meanwhile Saul was growing mad with jealousy. He hated the bond of love between David and Jonathan, and in a rage he had eighty-five priests put to death, all because they had spoken well of David, and of his loyalty. David fled into the desert. There was now a state of war between him and Saul. Night and day the king searched for him but God kept him safe.

Twice David got the chance to kill Saul—once when they met in a lonely cave and again when he was lying asleep with his spear at his side, and all his bodyguards snoring around him. It would have been easy for David to murder the king, but he knew that whatever Saul had done, he was God's chosen ruler, and that God would deal with him in his own time.

In a great battle against the Philistines near Mount Gilboa, three of Saul's sons were killed, including Jonathan. The king himself was badly wounded, and he took his sword and killed himself.

David wept bitterly when he heard what had happened, and he wrote a lament for the dead king and his son:

Saul and Jonathan were lovely and pleasant in their lives, and in their death they were not divided; they were swifter than eagles, they were stronger than lions . . .

I am distressed for thee, my brother Jonathan: very pleasant hast thou been unto me: thy love to me was wonderful, passing the love of women.

How are the mighty fallen, and the weapons of war perished!

DAVID BECOMES KING

2 Samuel, 1 Chronicles 11, 14

Long ago Samuel had prophesied that David would one day become the king of Israel, and this came to pass. David asked God to guide him and the Lord sent him to Hebron, in the land of Judah.

It was a long time before David knew he was safe. Saul's followers gathered together and fought against him. But David's men steadily wore the enemy down.

The people honored David for his bravery and justice. They came to him and made him king over all Israel, and he marched to Jerusalem, conquered it, and named it the City of David. He became more and more powerful, because the Lord God Almighty was with him, and the king of Tyre built him a marvelous palace of cedar wood.

It was from King David that Jesus himself was descended, and that is why he would be called the Son of David.

BATHSHEBA

2 Samuel 11–12

King David had two wives already, but he fell in love with a third woman. Her name was Bathsheba, and she was very beautiful. Her husband's name was Uriah.

Because he was king, David was used to having whatever he wanted, and he wanted Bathsheba. There was a war at that time, and David gave orders that Uriah was to be sent into battle where the fighting was fiercest, and the poor man was killed. Bathsheba wept when she heard that her husband was dead, but she was now free to marry the king. She became his wife and bore him a son, but God was displeased with what David had done. He sent a man named Nathan to the king, to tell him this story:

"In a certain town there were once two men, one rich and one poor. The rich man had no end of sheep and cattle, but the poor man had nothing except this one ewe lamb. He raised it just like a child and it drank from his cup and slept in his arms. It was like a daughter to him.

"A traveler came to stay in the town, and the rich man, for all his wealth, gave him nothing. The poor man slaughtered his precious ewe lamb, so the stranger could have a meal."

David grew very angry when he heard this story. "The rich man deserves to die, and he must pay for the lamb four times over!" he said. "He showed no pity at all."

Then Nathan pointed at him. "You are that man!" he said. "God gave you everything and would have given you more besides, but you murdered Uriah because you wanted his wife. Because you have done this your newborn son will die."

And it happened exactly as Nathan had foretold. The child born to Bathsheba lived only seven days. But God still showed mercy to David. She had another son, whom they named Solomon, which means "loved by the Lord," and he grew up to be a great and wise ruler.

ABSALOM

2 Samuel 15–18

Of all David's sons Absalom was the best loved. He was praised for his beauty throughout Israel. He had fine thick hair and his body had no mark or blemish.

Absalom was proud. He was flattered by the people who flocked to his side, and he started to behave as if he were the king. "If only I had power," he would say, "I would judge wisely."

His father allowed him to go back to Hebron, because he said that he wanted to worship the Lord there. And then Absalom sent messengers out declaring, "As soon as you hear the sound of the trumpet, say this: 'Absalom is king in Hebron.'"

David's servants warned him that Absalom was becoming powerful. There was now a state of war between father and son, and David was forced to set out with an army. He wept to think he was going out to fight his beloved son. Some of the people were loyal to him but others mocked, pelting him with dirt and stones, remembering how he himself had risen up against Saul. But David trusted in God, believing that he would comfort him in his distress.

The two armies came together in battle at last, both with thousands of men.

Although King David wanted to win, the last order he gave to his commanders was this: "Be gentle with Absalom, for my sake."

But Absalom, who was riding a mule, got his hair tangled up in the branches of a tree. The mule went trotting on, and as he hung there Joab, David's chief commander, took three javelins and plunged them into the young man's heart.

When David heard that Absalom had been killed he went into his room over the gateway and wept:

"O my son Absalom, my son, my son Absalom! Would God I had died for thee, O Absalom, my son, my son!"

PSALMS OF DAVID   Psalms 23, 51, 139

The Lord is my shepherd, I shall not be in want.
He makes me lie down in green pastures,
he leads me beside quiet waters,
he restores my soul.
He guides me in paths of righteousness
for his name's sake.

Even though I walk
through the valley of the shadow of death,
I will fear no evil,
for you are with me;
your rod and your staff,
they comfort me.

You prepare a table before me
in the presence of my enemies.
You anoint my head with oil;
my cup overflows.

Surely goodness and mercy will follow me
all the days of my life,
and I will dwell in the house of the Lord
forever.

Psalm 23

Psalm 51 was written after David had stolen Bathsheba to be his wife:

Have mercy on me, O God,
according to your unfailing love:
according to your great compassion
blot out my transgressions.
Wash away all my iniquity
and cleanse me from my sin . . .

O Lord, you have searched me
and you know me.
You know when I sit and when I rise;
you perceive my thoughts from afar . . .
Before a word is on my tongue
you know it completely, O Lord . . .

Where can I go from your Spirit?
Where can I flee from your presence?
If I go up to the heavens, you are there;
if I make my bed in the depths you are there.
If I rise on the wings of the dawn,
if I settle on the far side of the sea,
even there your hand will guide me,
your right hand will hold me fast.

If I say, "Surely the darkness will hide me
and the light become night around me,"
even the darkness will not be dark to you;
the night will shine like the day,
for darkness is as light to you.

From Psalm 139

Cleanse me with hyssop, and I shall be clean;
wash me, and I shall be whiter than snow . . .

Create in me a pure heart, O God,
and renew a steadfast spirit within me.
Do not cast me from your presence
or take your Holy Spirit from me.

From Psalm 51

KING SOLOMON

1 Kings 1–3

King David had had a long reign and his time on earth had been troubled. There had been so much fighting, so many deaths, and he had lost his precious Absalom. He grew old and very feeble and had to try to rule the kingdom from his bed. He became anxious about who was to be king after him. Solomon was the man God had chosen, and yet, as David lay dying, his son Adonijah set himself up as king instead, equipping himself with splendid chariots and horses.

David sent for Bathsheba, Solomon's mother. "I will fulfill the promise that I swore by the Lord God of Israel," he said to her. "Solomon will have my throne."

He gathered together his rulers and gave them careful orders, and Solomon was set on a mule and escorted to Gihon. Nathan the prophet and Zadok the priest went with him, and Zadok anointed him with holy oil. Then the trumpets sounded and all the people shouted, "Long live King Solomon!" There was much rejoicing, people danced and made music, and the ground shook under their feet.

When King David heard what had happened he praised God from his bed. "Praise be to the Lord God of Israel," he murmured. Adonijah was terrified now in case Solomon should have him killed, but the new king promised that no harm would come to him if he proved himself to be a good man.

When David knew that death was near he sent for Solomon and said, "Be strong, show yourself a man, and observe what the Lord your God requires."

So Solomon went away; he had hard work to do. His brother Adonijah still wanted the throne. In the end he had the man put to death, and his friends with him. Many people had been killed in Adonijah's quest for the throne, and Solomon wanted the house of David to be free from all the old bloodshed.

Most of all, he wanted to be wise. At Gibeon, where he had offered a thousand burnt offerings on the altar, God appeared to him in a dream. "I am young," he said to the Lord, "I am just a child. Give me wisdom in ruling over all these people."

And the Lord was pleased with him. "Because you have asked for wisdom above all else," he said, "I will give you riches and honor too. There will never have been a king like you, and if you walk in my ways, like your father, David, I will give you a long life."

Soon Solomon's wisdom was put to the test. Two women came to his court. They were quarreling over a baby. Both had given birth to children, but one baby had died. Now they were fighting over whom the living child belonged to. "It's mine," the first woman said. "No, it's mine," cried the other. "Your baby died."

"Bring me a sword," said King Solomon. "We will cut this baby in two and you can have half each."

The mother of the living child couldn't bear this. "Give him to the other woman," she said. "No, let him be cut in two," the second told Solomon.

But the king ruled that the baby should be given to its real mother, the one who loved the baby so much that she was willing to let the other woman have him if it would save his life. Israel marveled at the wisdom Solomon had shown.

THE WISDOM OF SOLOMON

Here are some of the proverbs of King Solomon.

My son, do not forget my teaching,
but keep my commands in your heart . . .
Let love and faithfulness never leave you;
bind them around your neck,
write them on the tablet of your heart.
Then you will win favor and a good name
in the sight of God and man.

Proverbs 3

When the storm has swept by, the wicked are
*   gone,*
but the righteous stand firm forever.

Proverbs 10

Reckless words pierce like a sword,
but the tongue of the wise brings healing.

Proverbs 12

He who fears the Lord has a secure fortress,
and for his children it will be a refuge.

Proverbs 14

A gentle answer turns away wrath,
but a harsh word stirs up anger.

Proverbs 15

Better a dry crust with peace and quiet
than a house full of feasting, with strife.

Proverbs 17

The Hebrew people taught their children through these wise sayings.

There is a time for everything,
and a season for every activity under heaven:
a time to be born and a time to die,
a time to plant and a time to uproot,
a time to tear down and a time to build,
a time to weep and a time to laugh,
a time to mourn and a time to dance . . .
a time to love and a time to hate,
a time for war and a time for peace.

Ecclesiastes 3

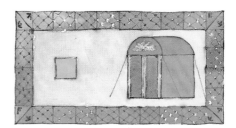

BUILDING THE TEMPLE

2 Samuel 7, 1 Kings 5–6

King David had wanted to build a house for God. He had said to Nathan the prophet, "Here I am, living in a splendid palace, while all my Lord God has is a tent." But God had told him that the task of building a temple was not his, that it would fall to his son Solomon. And this came true. Solomon built the temple, and it was a marvelous one.

God had kept his promise to him and he was very rich, so he was able to make everything of the very best, for the Lord. The temple was to be built of cedar wood. The timbers came from King Hiram of Tyre, who floated great logs by sea. In return Solomon sent food for his household—olive oil and wheat.

For the building, the king took workers from all over Israel. He needed stonecutters and carpenters, workers in gold and fine metals. The temple had two large rooms, the Holy Place and the Most Holy Place. The Most Holy Place was to house the ark of the Lord, and it was covered with gold. Everything was decorated with trees and flowers, and cherubim of gold and olive wood stood there.

Solomon's prayer for his temple was this: "When your people pray, O Lord, hear them, from heaven your dwelling place, hear them, and be merciful."

THE QUEEN OF SHEBA

1 Kings 10, 2 Chronicles 9

The Queen of Sheba had heard all about Solomon, and about how he trusted in God, and she came to visit him. She wanted to put him to the test and ask him some very hard questions. She did not arrive in Jerusalem alone but with a huge

procession of followers, and camels loaded with spices, gold, and jewels. She was much troubled, and she asked Solomon about God. Nothing was too hard for the king, and he explained everything to her.

When the queen heard his wise sayings and saw his marvelous palace, his servants, and the offerings he made each day to the Lord, she could hardly speak.

"I didn't believe what people said about you," she told him. "But in both wealth and wisdom you far exceed what I heard." And she praised the Lord for having set Solomon upon his throne.

Then she showered him with gifts, with spices and gold and jewels. People had never seen anything like it in their lives. He gave her presents, too, but more than that, he shared his wisdom with her.

Solomon ruled over his kingdom for forty years and was buried in Jerusalem, the city of his father, David.

ELIJAH AND THE WIDOW'S SON

1 Kings 17

Elijah was a prophet from Gilead. God had given him a special gift; he was able to look into the future and see what was going to happen.

One day, in a dream, Elijah saw that there would be no rain for months on end, and that there would be terrible famine. This was God's judgment upon the people for worshiping idols. Then he heard the voice of the Lord telling him to prepare for a very long journey. "Go east," it said, "until you find a little stream that flows near the River Jordan. It will provide water for you to drink, and I have commanded ravens to bring you food."

Elijah found the little stream and drank from it, and, sure enough, each morning and evening the ravens carried food down to him in their beaks.

But in the end even the little stream dried up, and Elijah grew thirsty. "Now go to the city of Zarephath," God commanded. "There is a woman living there who will look after you." So Elijah set off again and came at last to the gate of the city where he saw a poor woman gathering a few sticks to make a fire.

"Could you bring me some water," he asked her, "and a little food? I have walked so many miles today." But the woman said bitterly, "I have hardly any food left, only a handful of flour in a barrel, and a tiny drop of oil in a jar. These sticks are to make the fire for my very last meal. When that's gone I shall die, and so will my son."

"Don't be afraid," Elijah told her. "Go home and make your fire. But when the food is cooked bring me a little too. God has promised that your barrel of flour and your jar of oil will never be empty."

So she went home and did exactly what he told her. And it was true; there was always oil in the jar and flour in the barrel. God had kept his word.

But even though they now had enough to eat, her son fell ill, wasted away, and died. In her grief the poor woman turned on the stranger, Elijah. She blamed him. "Why did you bring this on me?" she wept. "Did you simply come here to remind me of the mistakes I've made in my life, and to punish me for them?"

Elijah gathered the boy in his arms, took him upstairs, and laid him on his own bed. Then he prayed to God long and hard. "Why has this awful thing happened," he asked, "to a poor woman who took me in, and looked after me? Dear Lord, bring her child to life again, I beg you."

And God heard his prayer. Very soon the boy started to breathe again, opened his eyes, and sat up. Elijah took him down to his mother. "He is alive," he said.

Then the woman held her son very tight, and turned to Elijah. "Now I know you are a true man of God," she said joyfully, "a special person through whom he shows his power and his love."

ELIJAH AND THE PROPHETS OF BAAL

1 Kings 18

In the days of King Ahab the Israelites had turned away from the Lord and were worshiping Baal and other false gods. Ahab knew that the prophet Elijah hated his wrongdoing. "You're a troublemaker," he told him. "No," said Elijah, "you are the one who is making trouble. Follow the Lord, if he is truly God; otherwise, follow Baal. But he is false."

The king called together his people on Mount Carmel, and Elijah gave them the same message. "Make up your minds: God or Baal," he said. But they gave him no answer.

"I am the only prophet the Lord has left," Elijah told them. "Baal has four hundred and fifty of them. Let us slaughter two bulls for sacrifice but not set fire to them. You call on Baal and I will call upon God. Whichever god sends down fire is the one we must worship."

So the people killed a bull and called on Baal from dawn till dusk. "Answer us!" they cried. But the heavens were silent.

Elijah taunted them. "Shout louder!" he said. "Your god might be busy, or on a journey. Or perhaps he's just asleep." So they shouted even louder and slashed themselves with swords so that blood ran down. But Baal answered not a word.

Then Elijah called the people around him. The altar of the Lord was in ruins, but he built it up again, placed his bull upon it, and ordered them to drench it with jars of water. Then he prayed to the Lord. "Answer me," he said, "so that these people may know you are truly God."

As he spoke flames licked around the altar, and the sacrifice was consumed by fire. The people fell on their faces crying, "The Lord is God!"

The prophets of Baal were put to death, and at last, after years of drought, God sent rain. At first people could see nothing, and then a tiny cloud appeared, only the size of a man's hand. Finally the clouds grew black and the heavens opened. God had heard his people, and been merciful.

THE STILL, SMALL VOICE

1 Kings 19

After the prophets of Baal had been put to death Elijah had to flee for his life. He knew that Ahab's followers hated him and would try to kill him in revenge. He went into the desert and prayed that he might die. "Lord, I have had enough," he said, and he lay down under a tree and went to sleep.

But God sent an angel to him with food and drink, a newly-baked loaf, and a pitcher of water. Strengthened by the food the Lord had provided, Elijah set off toward Mount Horeb where he spent the night in a cave.

While he was there God spoke to him. "What are you doing here, Elijah?" he said.

"I have been fighting for you, Lord," he answered. "The Israelites have turned away from you, and I am the only true prophet left. Now they are going to kill me."

"Go outside and stand on the mountainside," God told him. "The Lord is about to pass by."

Then a great wind blew and shattered the rocks, but the Lord was not in the wind. Then there was an earthquake, but the Lord was not in the earthquake. Then a fire raged around, but the Lord was not in the fire. After the fire came a still, small voice. When Elijah heard it he wrapped his cloak around his face, went to the mouth of the cave, and spoke with God.

A helper was provided for the lonely prophet. His name was Elisha, and Elijah found him plowing a field with some oxen. Elisha had no doubt that God meant him to follow Elijah. The prophet had thrown his cloak around Elisha as a sign that the young man would succeed him. Elisha kissed his father and mother goodbye, and set off with the prophet, to help him in his labors for God.

THE PARTING OF ELIJAH AND ELISHA

2 Kings 2

Elisha was true to Elijah; he went with him everywhere. But now the time had come for Elijah to make his very last journey. Elisha was with him, knowing that the end was near.

They were traveling from Gilgal and a crowd of prophets was following behind. "Did you know that the Lord is going to take away your master today?" they said to Elisha.

"Yes," he replied. "But do not speak of it." And he promised Elijah that he would never leave him.

When they reached the River Jordan the prophets stopped. But Elijah rolled up his cloak and struck the water with it. And the river divided to right and to left, letting them cross over to dry ground.

"What can I do for you, before I leave you?" Elijah asked Elisha.

"Give me your spirit, your power," was the reply.

"That is hard," said the old prophet. "But the gift will be yours if you see me when I am taken away."

And as they walked and talked together, a chariot of fire appeared, pulled by two blazing horses, separating the two men. Elijah was carried up to heaven in a whirlwind while Elisha cried, "My father! My father! The chariots and horsemen of Israel!" But Elijah had vanished, and Elisha tore at his clothes in grief.

ELISHA'S MIRACLES

2 Kings 4–5

When Elijah went up to heaven in his fiery chariot, his cloak had fallen to the ground. Elisha picked it up, and knew that his master had passed on his power. Soon Elisha started to work miracles, just like Elijah. One was for a poor widow whose children were about to be taken away as slaves. Their father had died, leaving bad debts.

"Go to your neighbors and collect empty jars from them," Elisha told her. "Then go home and fill all the jars with oil." The widow obeyed, and although she'd started with only a few drops of oil the jars kept filling up, right up to the brim. It was a miracle.

"All will be well now," said Elisha. "You can sell the oil and pay what you owe. No one will take away your children."

Another of Elisha's miracles was to heal a leper. This was Naaman, a commander in the king of Syria's army. All thought well of him because he had gained victory for his master. But the poor man suffered from the hideous disease of leprosy.

His wife had an Israelite slave girl who had heard all about Elisha. "He could cure your husband," she said.

The Syrian king wrote a letter to the king of Israel, and sent Naaman off with it, bearing gifts of gold and silver and fine clothing. The letter said, "Please heal my servant."

But the king of Israel tore helplessly at his robes. "What am I to do?" he cried. "Am I God? The king of Syria is just trying to make trouble."

Elisha heard what had happened and knew he could help. He sent a message. "Tell Naaman to come to me," it said, "so that he will know there is a prophet in Israel."

Up galloped Naaman to the prophet's door, in a whirl of horses and chariots. But Elisha did not come out to meet him. Instead he sent out a servant with a message: "Wash yourself seven times in the River Jordan," it said, "and you will be healed."

Naaman felt insulted that Elisha had not come out in person. "Besides, the rivers of Damascus are every bit as good as the Jordan," he shouted, and he stormed off.

But his servants persuaded him to do as he'd been told, so he went and dipped himself in the river. And he was healed.

Full of thanks, Naaman tried to give Elisha expensive presents. The prophet refused them, but his servant Gehazi ran after the chariots, begging for money and fine clothes. His greed angered Elisha. "Is this the time to accept gifts?" he asked. "From now on you and your family will suffer from leprosy, like Naaman." And as the servant turned away, his skin suddenly became as white as snow.

JEHU AND JEZEBEL

2 Kings 9–10

The kingdom of Israel was now split into two. One was called Israel, the other Judah. The rulers of Israel, King Ahab and Queen Jezebel, were wicked people. Jezebel had murdered the prophets of the Lord, and both had worshiped the false god Baal. To deal with them, and to carry on Elisha's work, God raised up a man named Jehu. He was a great charioteer, and he drove faster than the wind. God's plan was that Jehu should wipe out the whole family of wicked King Ahab.

But when Jezebel heard that Jehu was coming, she painted her face, did her hair, and peered down at him from a window. Jehu was not fooled by her beauty. He had her thrown down, and her blood spattered the walls as she fell. There was nothing left to bury; the dogs devoured her, just as the prophet Elijah had said. And Jehu had obeyed God, in destroying those who had worshiped Baal.

JOASH, THE BOY KING

2 Kings 11

Another great man raised up by God was a mere boy named Joash. His grandmother, the evil Queen Athaliah, decided to rule the kingdom of Judah herself. Her son, King Ahaziah, had been killed by Jehu. So she set about destroying the rest of the royal family. But the little prince Joash was saved, hidden with his nurse in the temple for six years while Athaliah was on the throne.

In the seventh year of the wicked queen's reign, Jehoida the priest decided to show Joash to the people. He summoned the temple guards and gave them the spears and shields of King David himself. Then he crowned Joash and proclaimed him king. "Long live the king!" the people shouted. Trumpets were blown and there was great rejoicing, but Queen Athaliah cried, "Treason! Treason!"

She was put to death for her wickedness, and young Joash took his seat on the royal throne. He was just seven years old, and he ruled in Jerusalem for forty years. He was a righteous man, and he walked with God.

JOSIAH AND THE LOST BOOK OF THE LAW

2 Kings 22–23

Another boy king was Josiah; he was only eight years old when he came to the throne. He was a good king, and he did what was right in God's sight.

Like Joash before him, he made repairs to the temple, and it was then that the high priest found the Book of the Law. It had lain forgotten in the temple for centuries. The high priest gave it to the king's secretary, whose name was Shaphah. And Shaphah took the book to Josiah, and read it to him.

When the king heard God's law he was filled with grief and tore at his clothes. "The Lord's anger is great," he said, "because our forefathers turned away from him. They did not obey what is written in this book."

Then he sent for a prophetess named Huldah, and she said this: "The Lord will bring disaster on this place because its people have worshiped idols and strange gods. But because King Josiah is sorry he will be spared."

Then Josiah gathered his people together and promised the Lord that from then on his commandments would be kept. The shrines to Baal and to the sun and moon were smashed to pieces; so were the horses of the sun which stood at the temple gates. The tombs of the wicked priests were destroyed. Nothing was left except the tomb of Elisha, who had prophesied that all this would happen. Josiah did not allow Passover to be celebrated until every trace of false worship had been done away with. He had truly turned to God with all his heart and soul. There was never another king to compare with him.

WORDS OF THE PROPHETS

Amos 2, Hosea 6 & 11, Micah 4–6, Isaiah 43 & 53

AMOS the shepherd looked upon Israel and was angry that its people had become so greedy and selfish. God gave him these words to speak on his behalf:

Hear this word, O house of Israel,
this lament I take up concerning you . . .
Seek the Lord and live,
or he will sweep through the house of Joseph
*   like a fire . . .*
let justice roll on like a river,
righteousness like a never-failing stream!

HOSEA reminded people that God had always loved them, whatever had gone wrong:

Come, let us return to the Lord . . .
He has injured us
but he will bind up our wounds.
After two days he will revive us;
on the third day he will restore us,
that we may live in his presence . . .
He will come to us like the winter rains,
like the spring rains that water the earth.

When Israel was a child, God said, *I loved*
*   him,*
and out of Egypt I called my son.
But the more I called Israel,
the further they went from me.
They sacrificed to the Baals
and they burned incense to images.

It was I who taught Ephraim to walk,
taking them by the arms;
but they did not realize
it was I who healed them.
I led them with cords of human kindness,
with ties of love;
I lifted the yoke from their neck
and bent down to feed them.

MICAH told the people that one day there would be peace in the world, and that a shepherd king would rule over his people:

He will judge between many peoples
and will settle disputes for strong nations far and
*   wide.*
They will beat their swords into plowshares
and their spears into pruning hooks.
Nation will not take up sword against nation,
nor will they train for war anymore.

He will stand and shepherd his flock
in the strength of the Lord,
in the majesty of the name of the Lord his God.
And they will live securely, for then his greatness
will reach to the ends of the earth.
And he will be their peace.

He has showed you, O man, what is good.
And what does the Lord require of you?
To act justly and to love mercy
and to walk humbly with your God.

ISAIAH knew that God's love was very great. He told them what God wanted to say to them:

Fear not, for I have redeemed you;
I have summoned you by name;
you are mine.
When you pass through the waters,
I will be with you;
and when you pass through the rivers,
they will not sweep over you.
When you walk through the fire,
you will not be burned . . .
since you are precious and honored in my sight,
and because I love you,
I will give men in exchange for you,
and people in exchange for your life.

Isaiah knew that one day God would send his only son to die for the sins of mankind. This is how he described him:

a man of sorrows, and familiar with suffering . . .
He was pierced for our transgressions,
he was crushed for our iniquities;
the punishment that brought us peace was upon
*   him,*
and by his wounds we are healed.

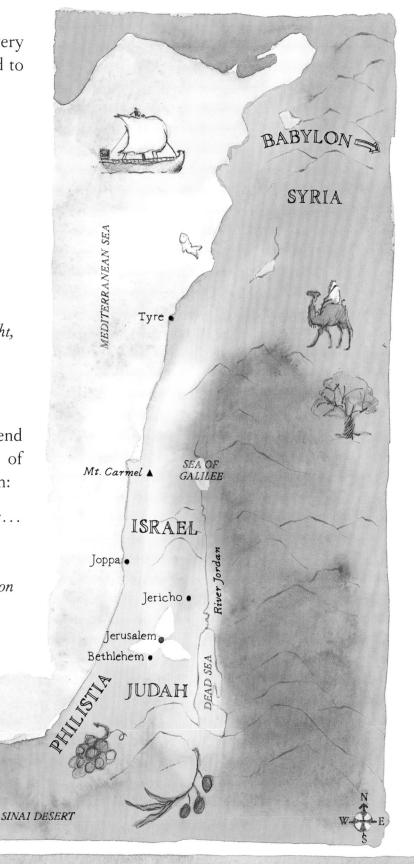

THE FALL OF JERUSALEM

2 Kings 24–25, Jeremiah 5 & 36–37

In a vision the prophet Jeremiah saw that Jerusalem would be destroyed. He told the people:

"This is what the Lord God Almighty says . . .
I am bringing a distant nation against you—
an ancient and enduring nation,
a people whose language you do not know,
whose speech you do not understand . . .
They will devour your harvests and food,
devour your sons and daughters . . .
With the sword they will destroy
the fortified cities in which you trust.'"

The prophet's words came true. In the reign of King Jehoiakim, who ruled over Jerusalem and did evil things in the sight of the Lord, God told Jeremiah to warn the people that they should repent of their evil ways and follow him again. The prophet obeyed, writing down his visions on a scroll. This was read aloud to King Jehoiakim, but he would not listen to God's voice. He cut the scroll into pieces and burned it on the fire.

When Jehoiakim died, his son Jehoiachin reigned instead. Then King Nebuchadnezzar of Babylon laid siege to the city of Jerusalem and forced the king and his court to give up all their power. He took Jehoiachin prisoner and carried away all the treasures of Jerusalem, both from the royal palace and from the temple, all the marvelous gold objects made by Solomon. Everyone was taken away into exile, the king and his family, the royal servants, the officers and the soldiers, the craftsmen. No one was left except the poor and helpless. And Nebuchadnezzar set up a new king in the city. His name was Zedekiah.

All this happened because the people had turned away from God. The Lord was angry with them.

Jeremiah had been beaten and thrown into prison but eventually Zedekiah sent for him. He was afraid of Nebuchadnezzar, and he knew Jeremiah was wise. "Is there any word from the Lord?" he wanted to know.

"Yes," said Jeremiah, "you are going to be handed over to the king of Babylon."

But Zedekiah's servant persuaded him that Jeremiah was too dangerous a man to be on the loose, and the soldiers were frightened at the thought of being attacked. So they took ropes and lowered Jeremiah into an empty well, and let him sink into the mud.

But the king still had faith in Jeremiah. He had him pulled up out of the well, and he talked with him. The prophet told him that he must surrender to the Babylonians when they attacked, and that if he refused he and all his family would perish.

But Zedekiah did not obey Jeremiah, and that is how the great city of Jerusalem fell. Nebuchadnezzar besieged it for four months, and the people began to starve. Then his soldiers broke through the city walls. Zedekiah's army escaped through a gate near the king's garden, but the Babylonians overcame them in the plains of Jericho. Zedekiah's sons were killed in front of him, then his eyes were gouged out and he was fettered with bronze shackles and dragged off to Babylon.

All the great buildings of Jerusalem were burned to the ground, the temple was looted and all its treasures taken away, and the priests and the doorkeepers were made prisoners.

And so the people of Judah, who had lived so long in Jerusalem, went into captivity, just as Jeremiah had foretold.

91

THE VISIONS OF EZEKIEL

Ezekiel

In the days of King Zedekiah, the prophet Ezekiel was living with the exiles in Babylon. But though he was far away from his own land, he had visions of it, and of God's plan for his people. He knew the Lord still loved them, even though they had turned away from him.

This is a vision Ezekiel had while he was living in Babylon, by the Kebar River:

A whirlwind came out of the north, a huge flashing cloud surrounded by brilliant light. In the center it glowed, like hot metal, and I saw four living creatures in the midst. They were shaped like humans, but each had four faces and four wings. The faces were those of a man, a lion, an ox, and an eagle. Fire flashed over them continually, and they moved this way and that, like streaks of lightning.

On the ground, next to each one, was a wheel, sparkling like chrysolite. Within each wheel was a second wheel. The rims were high and each studded with eyes.

Wherever the creatures went the wheels went with them. When the creatures stood still the wheels stood still too, because the spirit of the creatures lived inside them.

A vast sheet spread out over these creatures, something vast and terrifying, that sparkled like ice, and when they moved their wings it sounded like the rushing of great waters, like the voice of Almighty God.

I heard a voice coming out of a great brightness, light that shone like a rainbow through the rain. And I fell on my face.

The voice told me to take the words of the Lord to the rebellious people of Israel, and a hand stretched out, giving me a scroll on which were written words of despair and sorrow. "Eat this scroll," said the voice, "then go to the house of Israel." So I ate, and in my mouth it tasted as sweet as honey.

Then Ezekiel had another vision. This too was about the exiled children of Israel, and in it God took him into a great valley littered with dry bones:

"Can these bones come to life?" the Lord said to me.

"Only you know that," was my answer.

And God made me speak to the dry bones in the valley. "Tell them," he said, "that I will breathe into them and bring them to life. I will cover them with muscles and flesh and skin, and they will live again. Then they will know that I am the Lord."

So I did what God had said, and as I spoke I heard a rattling sound. There were the bones, coming together just as I had been told. But there was no life in them.

Then the Lord commanded me to summon the four winds of the earth, to breathe into the dead and give them life. So I did what he said, and the bones became people, standing up on their feet, a great army of them.

God said to me, "These bones are the house of Israel. They say to me, 'We are dried up, we are cut off, all our hope is gone.' But I am telling them this: 'I am going to bring you back from the dead and take you home to your own country. I will put my Spirit in you and you will live again. Then you will know that I am the Lord.'"

THE SONG OF THE EXILES

Psalm 137

This is the song of the people of Judah, mourning in exile over all they had lost:

By the rivers of Babylon, there we sat down, yea we wept, when we remembered Zion.

We hanged our harps upon the willows in the midst thereof.

For there they that carried us away captive required of us a song; and they that wasted us required of us mirth, saying, "Sing us one of the songs of Zion."

How shall we sing the Lord's song in a strange land?

If I forget thee, O Jerusalem, let my right hand forget her cunning.

If I do not remember thee, let my tongue cleave to the roof of my mouth; if I prefer not Jerusalem above my chief joy.

BELSHAZZAR'S FEAST

Daniel 5

Nebuchadnezzar's son Belshazzar was now the king of Babylon, and he too turned away his face from God and worshiped idols.

One day he gave a great feast for a thousand people. They drank wine out of the gold and silver goblets which his father had stolen from the temple in Jerusalem, and as they drank they praised the gods of silver and gold, of iron, wood, and stone.

But suddenly the fingers of a human hand appeared and wrote something on the palace wall. Belshazzar turned pale with fright, his knees knocked together, and he sagged down. Magicians were sent for and were promised riches and power, if only they could tell him what the strange writing meant. But no one could help, so he sent for his wise men. They didn't understand the writing either.

Then his wife told him about Daniel, one of the exiles. "Send for him," she said. "He can interpret dreams and riddles." So Belshazzar sent for him. "I will give you a purple robe and a gold chain," he said, "and the highest office in my kingdom too, if only you will help me."

But Daniel did not want the king's gifts. He told Belshazzar all about his father, Nebuchadnezzar, and how, because of his cruelty and pride, he had lost all he owned and been driven into the desert, where he'd eaten grass like the cattle.

"You have not humbled yourself like that," he went on. "You have set yourself up against God, using his holy vessels for your own pagan feasts. God sent that hand to warn you, and this is what it says:

MENE, MENE, TEKEL, PARSIN —

"This is what it means:

God has brought your reign to an end.

He weighed you in his scales and you have been found wanting.

Your kingdom has been split between the Medes and the Persians."

Belshazzar insisted on giving Daniel gifts, but it made no difference. That very night he was killed, and Darius the Mede became king instead.

THE FRIENDLY LIONS

Daniel 6

King Darius the Mede liked and trusted Daniel. He was planning to put him in charge of the whole kingdom. But the royal servants were deeply jealous; they were watching Daniel carefully.

Their problem was that he did nothing wrong at all, and they soon realized that the only way to get him into trouble was to make a new law to trap him. They knew that he was a righteous man, and faithful to his God, so they wrote out a special decree which said that from now on people could pray only to the king. Anyone who disobeyed would be thrown into a pit full of lions.

Now Daniel heard about this new law, but he paid no attention. Three times a day he went off to his house, opened the windows that looked toward Jerusalem, fell on his knees, and prayed. The jealous servants spied on him, then rushed off to tell the king what they had seen. "Doesn't the new law say that prayers may only be offered to you," they asked slyly, "and that anyone who disobeys must be thrown to the lions?"

"It is true," admitted King Darius, though his heart was heavy. "It does say that, and a royal law cannot be changed."

"Well, Daniel is paying no attention," they informed him. "He prays to God three times a day. We've seen him."

When the king heard this he was very unhappy, because he loved and honored Daniel, and all day he thought hard for some way to save him.

And from deep in the pit a voice rang out. "O King, may you live forever. In the night God sent his angels to shut the lions' mouths. He knew that I was innocent."

But the jealous servants came back again and told Darius firmly that the new law could not be changed.

So Darius gave orders for Daniel to be thrown to the lions. "But may your God, whom you serve so faithfully, save you now," he said, as Daniel was dragged away from the palace to the deep pit where the savage creatures were waiting.

The servants rolled a huge stone over the entrance, and the king came and marked it with his own special ring, to show that no one must break in. Then he went back to his palace. For the rest of the day he neither ate nor drank, and he sent away his court musicians. All night he lay tossing and turning, and thinking about Daniel.

In the morning Darius ran straight to the pit and called out in fear, "Daniel, servant of the living God, has the one whom you served so faithfully been able to save you from the jaws of the lions?"

In joy Darius ordered his men to bring Daniel out of the pit. They could find no marks on him at all. That was because he had trusted in God with his whole heart to save him.

As for the jealous servants, they were thrown into the pit themselves. Even before they had reached the bottom the lions sprang up and devoured them.

And Darius wrote a grand decree, ordering everyone to fear and honor Daniel's God. "For he is the living God," it said. "His kingdom shall last forever and ever."

The Temple is Rebuilt

Ezra, Nehemiah

For many years the Jews, the people of Judah, had been in exile in Babylon. They missed their country and they missed worshiping in the great temple at Jerusalem.

But then something marvelous happened. A Persian king named Cyrus conquered Babylon and decided to let the Jews go home. His heralds made a proclamation: "God has appointed King Cyrus to have the temple at Jerusalem rebuilt. Any of his people may go and build it, and may their God be with them."

So some of the Jews set off for Jerusalem, and set about rebuilding their temple. As they worked the priests praised the Lord with trumpets and cymbals. "The Lord is good," they sang. "His love for Israel endures forever."

But the older priests, remembering how glorious the old temple had been, wept aloud.

Now the Jews had enemies who did not want the temple rebuilt. To them the very name Jerusalem spelled nothing but trouble. From that city people had rebelled against kings and overthrown them. So the work on the temple came to a halt.

Then men of God rose up to help the Jews—two prophets named Haggai and Zechariah—and they got the work started again. King Darius was on the throne now, and he too wanted the temple rebuilt. His royal decree commanded that all the gold and silver that Nebuchadnezzar had stolen from the treasury was to be brought back, and that anyone who hampered the rebuilding was to be punished.

So at long last the temple was finished. It was dedicated to God, and the feast of the Passover was celebrated again. Then a great priest named Ezra arrived in Jerusalem, a righteous man on whom God's hand had rested. He was put in charge of refurnishing the temple and of appointing judges to rule over the people. So he brought back the Jewish families who had remained in Babylon and led them toward their temple.

But they had not quite forsaken their old ways. They had broken God's laws. At this Ezra wept and tore at his clothes, and the people wept with him. But he did not forget to thank God for his mercy. "You have punished us far less than our sins deserve," he said. "And we are guilty. None of us can stand in your presence."

NEHEMIAH REBUILDS THE CITY WALLS

Nehemiah 1–6

The Jews had rebuilt their temple in Jerusalem, but the city itself was in ruins. The walls had been broken down and the great gates burned to cinders.

Nehemiah, a Jewish cupbearer in the court of King Artaxerxes, was sick at heart. One day, when he took the king his cup of wine, the king noticed how sad he looked, and asked him what the matter was.

"The city of my fathers lies in ruins," Nehemiah said. "Let me go back to Jerusalem and help to rebuild it." And the king let him go.

Nehemiah waited until nightfall, and then he rode around the city on a donkey and inspected the city walls. There was no doubt in his mind when he saw them. The whole city must be rebuilt. So he gathered people together to help him.

The Sheep Gate was rebuilt by Eliashib, the high priest. The Fish Gate was rebuilt by the sons of Hassenaah. Then they mended the Jeshanah Gate, the Valley Gate, and the Dung Gate. Shallun rebuilt the Fountain Gate with a roof, bolts, and bars. Then he mended the wall by the Pool of Siloam. Little by little the great city was rising again from its ruins.

But the Jews had enemies who mocked them. "What are these pathetic people doing?" someone shouted. "Can they bring life back into heaps of rubble? If a mere fox climbed up on these walls of theirs they would collapse."

Nehemiah ignored them. He prayed to God for help and went on rebuilding the city. Soon it was half done, because the people were working night and day.

They were frightened though. "We are going to be attacked," they told Nehemiah.

But he reassured them, putting people with weapons at the lowest points of the wall, and encouraging them not to be afraid. "Remember that the Lord is great," he told them. And from then on the builders worked on the wall with swords at their side. They held on to their weapons from dawn until the first stars came out, and they slept in their clothes.

"Lord, strengthen my hands," Nehemiah prayed. And in fifty-two days the new wall was finished.

ESTHER

Esther

Queen Vashti, the wife of King Ahasuerus, was in disgrace. Her husband had summoned her to one of his splendid banquets, and she had refused to go. She was holding a banquet of her own, for the women of the court. Besides, all Ahasuerus wanted to do was to brag about her beauty.

But her refusal was seen as a terrible insult. The nobles feared that all their wives would start pouring scorn on them. And so Vashti was punished and sent away. Ahasuerus took a new queen named Esther. She was very young and

very beautiful and she was Jewish. Her parents were dead, and she had been brought up by a cousin named Mordecai.

Esther did not enter the king's presence for twelve months. The rule was that a new wife had to be prepared and made as attractive as possible with perfumes and costly oils. When the time came she was allowed anything she wanted, to take with her to the court. In her modesty, Esther asked for nothing, and this pleased King Ahasuerus. He put a crown on her head and proclaimed a holiday. She was his favorite.

Meanwhile, Mordecai discovered that there was a plot to kill the king. He told Esther, she told her husband, and the men were hanged. This was all written down in the royal diary.

At court there was an arrogant, boastful man named Haman. Everyone had to bow down to him because Ahasuerus favored him highly, but Mordecai refused.

Haman was furious. It was not enough to kill Mordecai, he said. He would kill every single Jew. And he persuaded the king to send out orders for this to be done. The cruel commands were copied out and sent all over the kingdom. All Jews were to be killed—young and old, men, women, children.

When Mordecai heard about it he wept and tore his clothes. He could not go into the royal court himself but he sent a message to Esther, begging her to plead with the king, to change his mind. But the royal laws were strict. Ahasuerus had many wives, and none, not even Esther, could go to him without being sent for. The penalty for disobeying this was death.

But Mordecai would not give up. "If you say nothing," he warned, "the Jews may be saved some other way, but you and your family will die. Perhaps you are in this royal court for a purpose. Speak to the king."

Esther was convinced. "I shall break the law and tell him," she said, "and if I die, I die."

But she was patient. For three days she fasted and prayed, and she prepared a banquet for the king, in honor of Haman, his favorite. The foolish man went around boasting. "I'm the only one Queen Esther has invited to her feast," he said. "But I hate the sight of Mordecai sitting at the palace gate. I shall have a gallows built, to hang him on." And that is exactly what he did.

That night Ahasuerus could not sleep. So he decided to read the royal diary. There he discovered that Mordecai had saved him from two murderers. He wanted to thank him. So he sent for Haman. "What should be done for a man whom the king wants to honor?" he asked. Haman thought Ahasuerus was talking about him. "Let them lead him through the streets in a royal robe on a royal horse," he said. But he was ordered to do this for Mordecai, whom he hated. When the procession was over he went home and wept, he was so jealous.

The banquet took place, and only then did Esther tell the king that she was a Jew. Only then did she ask him to spare her people. And she told the king how the cruel plot against them was all Haman's doing.

Ahasuerus wasted no time. Haman was hanged on the great gallows he had prepared for Mordecai, and Mordecai was brought before the king and given his own ring. Thanks to Esther's pleading, new royal commands were sent all over the kingdom. These said that if anyone tried to attack the Jews they were allowed to defend themselves. And they did.

There was much rejoicing when the news was known, and Mordecai went away from the royal court wearing a crown, dressed in purple fit for a king.

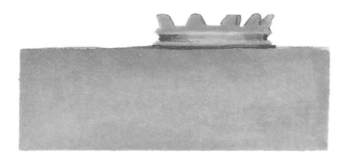

JONAH AND THE GREAT FISH

Jonah

Not all God's prophets obeyed him. One who didn't was named Jonah. God wanted him to go to Nineveh because its people were wicked. But Jonah ran away to the port of Joppa and boarded a boat bound for the remote city of Tarshish. He was determined to get away from God.

God raised a terrible storm, and the sailors were petrified. Each cried for help to his own god, and they threw out the cargo to try to stop the boat from sinking. Jonah was fast asleep below deck, but the captain shook him awake. "Call on your god," he pleaded. "Perhaps he'll listen to you."

Then the sailors cast lots, to find out who it was who'd brought the storm upon them. The lot fell upon Jonah, and they asked him a string of questions. "Who are you," they asked, "and where do you come from? What people do you belong to?"

"I am a Hebrew," he told them. "The God I worship made the land and the sea."

This frightened them. Jonah had already told them that he was running away from God. "How can we get the storm to die down?" they asked.

Jonah told them to throw him overboard. "This storm is all my fault," he said. They tried to row back to land, but as they struggled the sea grew even wilder. In the end they did as Jonah had said, and threw him over the side, begging God to spare them for drowning an innocent man. And at once the storm died away.

But Jonah did not drown. He was swallowed up by a great fish that God had sent, and he was in it for three days and three nights.

Deep inside the fish Jonah prayed to God:

"In my distress I called to the Lord,
and he answered me.
From the depths of the grave I called for help,
and you listened to my cry . . .
When my life was ebbing away,
I remembered you, Lord,
and my prayer rose to you,
to your holy temple."

After three days God gave a command to the huge fish. It opened its mouth, and Jonah stepped out onto dry land.

Then God ordered him a second time to go to Nineveh, and this time Jonah obeyed. He told the people that their city would be destroyed in forty days, and they went into mourning. The king decreed that everyone was to stop eating, as a sign that they were sorry, that everyone must give up their evil ways and listen to God again. "He may show mercy, even now," he said.

And God did. Seeing that they were truly sorry, he turned away his anger and forgave them.

Jonah was angry. "Isn't this just what I said before I set off?" he exclaimed. "I knew you were a loving God, slow to anger and a God of great mercy. That is why I set out for Tarshish. I knew you would not destroy Nineveh. Take away my life, Lord. I may as well be dead."

But God said, "What right have you to be angry?"

Jonah said nothing. He went outside the city and sat down to see what was going to happen. God caused a vine to grow, to protect him from the blazing sun, and Jonah was grateful.

The very next day, though, a worm came and destroyed the vine so that it withered away. Then an east wind blew and scorched Jonah's head. Again he pleaded with God, saying, "Let me die."

"Do you have any right to be angry about the vine?" God asked him.

"Yes," said Jonah.

But God showed him that he was mistaken. "You cared about the vine," he said, "a thing that just grew up overnight. You'd not planted it, or watered it, and yet you cared. So why should I not be concerned about the great city of Nineveh. It has a hundred and twenty thousand people in it who do not know their right hand from their left, and many cattle too. Should I not love them, Jonah, as I love you?"

The Lord is one

104

The New Testament

But one day God sent Gabriel, the great angel, to give Mary some very important news. She was troubled when she saw him, and wondered what he could want with her.

"Greetings, most favored one," he said, "and do not be afraid. God has chosen you out of all women. Very soon you are going to have a baby. You must call him Jesus. He will be great, the Son of the Most High. God will give him the throne of David, his mighty ancestor, and he will reign forever and ever."

But Mary was puzzled. "I am not even married," she told the angel.

"The Holy Spirit will come down to you," Gabriel said, "and God's own power will rest upon you; therefore, the holy child you will bear shall be called the Son of God, for God is his Father."

"I am his servant," Mary whispered. "May it happen just as you have said." And Gabriel went away.

Then Mary lifted up her voice and rejoiced:

"My soul glorifies the Lord.
Rejoice, my soul, in God my Savior,
who has looked so tenderly
upon his humble servant.
For from this day
all people shall call me blessed,
the Lord has dealt with me so
    wonderfully."

MARY'S WONDERFUL NEWS

Luke 1

There once lived, in the town of Nazareth, a young girl named Mary. She was soon going to marry a carpenter named Joseph.

JOHN THE BAPTIST

Matthew 3, Mark 1, Luke 3, John 1, Isaiah 40

Long ago the prophet Isaiah had written:

A voice of one who calls in the desert,
"Prepare the way for the Lord.
The crooked roads shall be made straight,
the rough places smooth.
And all people will see God's salvation."

Now this "voice" was the voice of John the Baptist, the cousin of Jesus, who was born when his mother, Elizabeth, was an old woman.

The angel Gabriel who visited Mary had first appeared to Elizabeth's husband, Zechariah the priest, and told him his wife would bear him a son. He was to be named John, and he was going to be the messenger of the Lord.

Zechariah refused to believe him. "My wife is too old," he said.

"I stand in the presence of God," Gabriel told him. "Because you have not believed my words you will be unable to speak from this moment on." And Zechariah was struck dumb. He went out of the temple but could only make signs to people. They realized he had had a vision.

When the baby was born everyone wanted to name him Zechariah, after his father. But his mother said, "No. He is to be called John." And his father, who still couldn't speak, wrote down the name for them. Then the Holy Spirit filled Zechariah. His speech came back and he uttered a prophecy:

"And you, child, will be called
a prophet of the Most High,
for you will go before the Lord,
to prepare his way."

When John grew up he became a great preacher. Crowds of people came to him to be baptized. He lived very strictly, wearing clothes of camel's hair and eating nothing but locusts and wild honey. His message was always the same: "Repent of your sins. The kingdom of heaven is very near. Lead holy lives, because those who do not will be cut down like rotten trees, and thrown into the fire."

He told people that Jesus was coming soon, and was a much greater man than he. "I am not worthy to stoop down and unlace his sandals," he said.

The Birth of Jesus

Luke 2

Only a few days before her baby was born, Mary had to go on a long journey with Joseph the carpenter. Everyone had been ordered to go to their hometown and pay a special tax there. Joseph's home was in Bethlehem.

Just as they arrived Mary knew that her baby was about to be born; but there was no room for them in the inn. All they were offered was a stable, and that is where the Son of God was born. There was no lovely silk-lined crib for him, only a manger full of hay, with the animals standing around.

That night some shepherds, who were out guarding their sheep on the hills near Bethlehem, were startled by a great light in the sky. An angel came down and told them not to be afraid. "I bring you good news of great joy," he said, "news for everyone on earth. Jesus Christ the Lord has been born tonight. If you go now, you will find him wrapped in swaddling bands, lying in a manger."

And suddenly the whole sky was filled with angels, hundreds upon thousands of them, all praising God. "Glory to God in the highest," they sang, "and on earth peace, good will toward all people."

"Come," the shepherds said to one another, when the angels had gone away. "Let's go to Bethlehem and see for ourselves." So they hurried away and found Mary and Joseph, and the baby Jesus lying in a manger, exactly as the angel had said.

THE WISE MEN

Matthew 2

Meanwhile, in his great palace in Jerusalem, jealous King Herod was talking to some wise men from the east. He had heard about the baby who had been born in Bethlehem and he was terrified that the child would one day seize the throne. The prophets had said that a great king, the Messiah, would be born in that little town where King David himself had been born.

"Where is this baby who is going to be king of the Jews?" the wise men asked Herod. "We have seen his special star in the east and we want to go and worship him."

"You'll find him in Bethlehem," Herod said. Then he added cunningly, "But be sure to let me know when you find him there. I want to come and worship him too."

So off they went, following the star; and it guided them all the way to Bethlehem and the place where Jesus lay. They were overjoyed to see the star there, and they went straight into the stable. Out of their great store of treasures they gave the baby three very special gifts, gold and frankincense and myrrh. But they were not so foolish as to return to Herod. In a dream God warned them to find a different way home.

HEROD IS ANGRY

Matthew 2, Luke 2, Jeremiah 31

One night, while Jesus was still a baby, Joseph had a dream. God sent an angel to give him a warning. "Go to Egypt," he said, "and stay there until I tell you that it is safe to come back. King Herod is mad with jealousy. He is plotting to kill your baby son."

So Joseph got up at once and stole away by night with Mary and their little child, to the far-off land of Egypt.

Meanwhile Herod flew into a great rage when he realized the wise men had tricked him. He commanded that all the young children in and around Bethlehem should be killed. That way he could be certain that the infant king would die too.

So all the babies were murdered, and the ancient words of Jeremiah the prophet came true:

A voice is heard in Ramah,
mourning and great weeping,
Rachel weeping for her children
and refusing to be comforted,
because her children are no more.

But Joseph and Mary were already safe in Egypt, and they did not go back to their own country until Herod was dead and they knew it was safe. Then they settled in the town of Nazareth.

When Jesus was still a baby they took him into the temple in Jerusalem. There, two elderly people, Simeon and Anna, were overjoyed to see him. They knew for certain that this was God's Son.

Simeon had been waiting a long time. He was an old man, but he knew that he would not die until he had held Jesus in his arms.

"Lord, now let your servant depart in peace," he said. "For my eyes have seen your salvation."

But he also told Mary and Joseph that Jesus would suffer. "A sword shall pierce your own soul too," he said to Mary.

Anna, the prophetess, was over eighty years old, but she was in the temple every day, fasting and praying. She too thanked God for Jesus' birth. She knew he had come to save the people of Israel.

Mary and Joseph took Jesus home. As he grew he was filled with wisdom, and the grace of God was upon him.

THE BOY JESUS IN THE TEMPLE

Luke 2

When Jesus was twelve years old, Mary and Joseph went up to Jerusalem as usual, for the great feast of the Passover, and they took their son with them. When it was all over they set off for home again, traveling with a big group of friends and family; but Jesus stayed behind. They had gone a whole day's journey before they realized he was missing. Then they began to hunt anxiously among the crowd. But Jesus was nowhere to be found.

Off they trudged, all the way back to Jerusalem. But it was a big, bustling city, and they spent three days looking for him. Finally they found him in the temple, sitting in the middle of the scholars and teachers, asking all kinds of questions, listening carefully to their answers and answering their questions too. Everyone who heard him was amazed at his deep understanding, and at how much such a young boy knew.

His parents were astonished to find him there, and Mary could not hide her distress.

"My son," she said, "why have you treated us like this? Your father and I have been terribly worried; we've looked everywhere for you."

JESUS IS BAPTIZED

Matthew 3 & 4, Mark 1 & 6, Luke 3

When Jesus came from Galilee to the River Jordan he asked his cousin John the Baptist to baptize him too. But John was unsure. He knew that Jesus was the greater man. "I am the one who needs to be baptized by you," he said. "Why are you coming to me?"

But Jesus said, "Baptize me. It is right for us to do this."

"But why did you look for me?" Jesus asked them. "Didn't you know that I had to be in my Father's house, doing my Father's work?" But Mary and Joseph did not understand what he was saying.

Together they all went home to Nazareth. But Mary never forgot what had happened in the temple, and treasured the memory in her heart.

As for Jesus, he grew taller and stronger, and he grew in wisdom too. People loved him, but no one loved him so much as his Father in heaven, in whose house he had lingered when he was just twelve years old.

So John went down with him into the waters of the Jordan and baptized him there. As Jesus came out again he saw that the heavens had opened. The Spirit of God had come down upon him in the form of a dove, which was resting on him. Then he heard a voice:

"This is my beloved Son, in whom I am well pleased."

Some time later John the Baptist met a cruel end. Herod was on the throne, the son of the king who had tried to kill the baby Jesus. John was a fearless man and brave enough to tell King Herod he was doing wrong to marry Herodias, the wife of his brother Philip. Herod was angry and he had John thrown into prison.

Herodias was even angrier—so angry in fact that she wanted Herod to have John killed. But the king knew he was a righteous man and he liked to hear him talk, so he did nothing about it.

Then Herod's birthday came around, and he gave a great feast for all the important people in his kingdom. Herodias saw her chance and sent in her daughter, Salome, to dance before the dinner guests. Herod was so enchanted by her that he offered her gifts. "You can have anything you want," he promised rashly. "You can have half my kingdom."

The girl went away and found her mother. "What shall I ask for?" she said.

"Ask for the head of John the Baptist," was the answer.

Salome came straight back to Herod and told him what she wanted. Herod was grieved, but he was trapped now, because of the promise he'd made in front of all his guests. So he sent off his executioner to the prison, with orders to behead John the Baptist. The man soon returned, bearing the head on a platter.

The head was given to Salome, her reward for dancing before Herod, and she took it to her cruel mother. Then John's followers came to the palace, took away the body of their beloved master, and laid it in a tomb.

IN THE WILDERNESS

Matthew 4, Luke 4

Soon after he had been baptized by his cousin John, Jesus went away into the wilderness. And the devil came to him there. Jesus was hungry because he had fasted for forty days and forty nights, and the devil saw a way to trap him.

"Command that these stones turn into bread," he said.

But Jesus quoted the Scriptures to him:

"Man shall not live by bread alone but by every word that proceedeth out of the mouth of God."

So the devil tried a second time, taking him to Jerusalem and making him stand on the topmost pinnacle of the temple. "If you really are the Son of God, throw yourself down from here," he said. "No harm can come to you." And he too quoted the Scriptures:

"He shall give his angels charge concerning thee: and in their hands they shall bear thee up, lest at any time thou dash thy foot against a stone."

But Jesus told him something else the Scriptures had said, that God must not be put to the test.

The devil did not give up. He took Jesus up to the top of a high mountain and showed him all the kingdoms of the world and all their marvels. "This will be yours," he wheedled. "All you need to do is bow down and worship me."

Then Jesus grew angry. "Get away from me, Satan!" he cried. "This too is written in the Scriptures:

"Thou shalt worship the Lord thy God, and him only shalt thou serve."

And the devil went away. But then angels came and looked after Jesus in that rocky wilderness.

JESUS CALLS HIS FIRST DISCIPLES

Mark 1 & 3, Luke 5 & 6

Jesus was going all over Galilee telling the people some good news. "Repent of your sins," he said. "The kingdom of heaven is near."

One day, standing on the shores of the Sea of Galilee, with everyone crowding around him to hear him preach, he saw two boats. They had been left there by some fishermen who were busy washing their nets.

One of the boats belonged to a man called Simon. Jesus got into it and asked him to move away from the shore a little, and when he could see everybody he sat down and preached.

Then he told Simon to move out into the deeper water and to drop his nets over the side.

"But Master," said the fisherman, "we have been trying to catch fish all night and we've caught nothing. Still, I will let down my nets, since you ask me to."

He did, and there were so many fish that the nets began to break. Other fishermen were called over to help and their boats were filled up. The weight of the catch was so great they almost sank.

Then Simon knew that he was in the presence of the Son of God, and he fell to his knees. "Leave me, Lord," he begged. "I am a sinful man."

But Jesus raised him to his feet. "Don't be afraid," he said. "From now on you won't be catching fish, but men." Andrew his brother was there, and so were James and John, the sons of Zebedee. These were the very first disciples, the "fishers of men."

Later, Jesus called other people to follow him. He gave them power to heal the sick and to cast out evil spirits from people who were troubled. There were twelve in all, and these are their names:

Simon (to whom Jesus gave the name Peter), Andrew, James and John; Philip, Bartholomew, Matthew, Thomas; James the son of Alphaeus, Thaddaeus, Simon the Zealot and Judas Iscariot. All were faithful to Jesus except for Judas. One day he would betray his master in exchange for thirty pieces of silver.

THE FIRST MIRACLE

John 2

Soon after he had called together his disciples Jesus went with them to a wedding in Galilee, at a place called Cana. His mother, Mary, was a guest too.

Before feasting was over the hosts ran out of wine. Mary came to Jesus and told him what had happened. It was a terrible thing. No more wine at a wedding party!

At first Jesus did not seem to want to help. "Why involve me?" he said to his mother. "My time has not yet come."

But Mary went away and said to the servants, "Do whatever my son tells you."

Nearby there were six stone jars. They

were very big; some could hold thirty gallons. "Fill them with water," Jesus said to the servants, and they did, right up to the brim.

"Now take some of the water to the master of the feast," said Jesus. When the man tasted it he realized that it had turned into wine—not cheap wine either, but the very best that money could buy. "The good wine is usually served first," he told the bridegroom, "but you have kept back the best until now."

This was the very first miracle that Jesus ever performed, revealing his glory. And when they saw it, his disciples believed in him.

THE SERMON ON THE MOUNT

Matthew 5–7

One day, Jesus preached to the people from a mountainside. His disciples were with him, and they listened too. He said:

"Blessed are the poor in spirit;
for theirs is the kingdom of heaven.
*   Blessed are those who mourn;*
for they shall be comforted. . .
*   Blessed are the merciful;*
for they shall receive mercy.
*   Blessed are the pure in heart;*
for they shall see God.
*   Blessed are the peacemakers;*
for they shall be called the children of God."

Jesus told another parable about the ways people listened to his words. This was the story of the sower. Once, he said, a farmer went out to sow some seed. He went all over his land, scattering it from a basket. Some fell by the roadside, where birds swooped down and gobbled it up.

The foolish man chose to build on sand, and when the great storms came his house fell down with a terrible crash.

"People are like that," Jesus explained. "Those who listen to my words and do what I say are building on rock. Those who hear what I say and do nothing about it are building on sand."

Some fell on rocks, where there was not enough soil, and as soon as the plants sprang up they withered away again. They had no deep roots, so the hot sun scorched and killed them. Some of the seed fell among thorns, so as soon as the plants grew they were choked.

But some of the seed fell on good soil, and from this the farmer got a fine crop, many times greater than the seed he had sown.

Jesus explained this story to the people. He told them that the seed was really his message about God's kingdom. Sometimes the devil snatches the words away, like the birds by the roadside. Sometimes a person will hear the message with great joy but then forget about it, almost at once. These people are like the plants with shallow roots. The thorns that choked the plants are the worries and cares of the world that crowd out the word of God so it can't grow. But the seed that fell on good soil is like someone who hears the word and understands it.

Jesus used many parables to explain what the kingdom of God is like. At first, he said, it is like a tiny mustard seed, the smallest seed of all. When that seed grows, though, it's the largest of all plants, so big that the birds come and perch on its branches.

121

He said too that God's kingdom was like treasure buried in a field. If a man digs it up he hides it again. But then he goes off and buys the whole field, so that he can own the treasure too.

And Jesus said the kingdom of God was like a merchant looking for the best pearls. When he finds the most beautiful one of all, the pearl of great price, he sells everything he has to buy it.

People who find God's kingdom, Jesus said, do not hide the good news away, just as people with a lamp don't cover the light with a bowl, or put it under a bed. They put the lamp on a stand and let it shine out, so that everyone can see.

Jesus told many stories about things that were lost. He wanted the people to know how much God loved them, and how he would go on looking for them until they were found. So that if a woman with ten silver coins loses one she will light a lamp and carefully sweep her house

until she finds it again. When she has found it she will call her friends and neighbors to share in her joy. In heaven, Jesus said, the angels rejoice too, when a sinful person says they are sorry.

Often, he said, people reminded him of sheep, wandering and lost, not knowing where their shepherd had gone. If a man had as many as a hundred sheep, he told them, and one got lost, he would look everywhere until he had found it. And God would rejoice more over that one sheep than over the ninety-nine others who had stayed close to home.

One of the greatest parables of all is called "The Prodigal Son."

There was once a man, said Jesus, with two sons. One day the younger one said greedily, "I want my share of our inheritance, now." So the father gave him the money, and in no time he had spent it all on drinking and gambling.

But a famine came to the country where he'd gone to live. He grew hungry, so hungry he could have eaten the pig swill. That was his job now, looking after pigs.

He decided to go home. "I will say to my father, 'I have done wrong. Treat me like one of the servants.'"

But while he was still far off, his father saw him, ran out, flung his arms around his neck, and kissed him. "Bring the best robe," he said, "and kill the fatted calf. We are going to have a feast. The son I thought was dead has come home alive."

All this time the older son had been working on the farm. When he heard the music and dancing he was jealous. "I've worked for you all these years," he grumbled, "and you never killed a prize calf for me."

"My son," the father told him, "whatever I have is yours. But how could we not rejoice today, when your lost brother has been found again?"

That is how God feels, Jesus said, when someone is sorry, and comes home.

A MARVELOUS PICNIC

Matthew 14, Mark 6, Luke 9, John 6

Everyone wanted to meet Jesus and to hear his wonderful stories, and wherever he went huge crowds followed him. Once, when he had been talking to the people all day, he said to his disciples, "Let us go away by ourselves now, to some lonely place, so that you can all get some rest." So they set off in a boat.

But the people had rushed ahead of them, and the minute Jesus stepped ashore everyone crowded around eagerly. His heart filled with love for them; they were like sheep that had no shepherd. And although he was very tired he started preaching again.

The day wore on, and his disciples began to worry. "It is getting late," they said. "Send the people away now to the villages nearby, to buy themselves something to eat."

"You feed them," Jesus replied.

"How on earth can we buy food for so many?" Philip wanted to know. "There must be about five thousand people here." Then Andrew came up and said, "There's a lad here, Master, with five barley loaves and two fish. But that won't go very far."

"Make everyone sit down," Jesus commanded, so they all settled themselves on the grassy slopes.

Then he took the loaves and the fish, gave thanks to God, and passed the food to his disciples to share out. Everyone ate till they were satisfied, and at the end there were enough crumbs and bits of fish left over to fill twelve baskets. It was the most marvelous picnic ever.

A Storm

Matthew 14, Mark 6, John 6

Late in the afternoon on the day of the marvelous picnic, Jesus finally sent the people away. He told the disciples to get into their boat and sail home ahead of him, while he went into the hills to pray.

When evening came he was still alone. The boat was a long way from land by this time. The waves were crashing against the side of the boat, and the wind was howling. All night the disciples had to struggle to hold a steady course.

Early next morning, long before sunrise, Jesus came to find them, walking across the water. When they saw what he was doing they cried out in terror, "It's a ghost!" But he calmed them at once, saying, "Take heart, it is I. Do not be afraid."

Peter said, "Lord, if it really is you, command me to walk on the sea as well."

"Very well," Jesus replied. "Come." And he held out his hand.

So Peter climbed out of the boat and tried, like Jesus, to walk on the water. But when the wind began to buffet him this way and that, and the great waves hurled themselves at him, his courage failed and he began to sink. "Lord, save me!" he shouted. And Jesus immediately caught him by the hand, saying, "Peter, how little your faith is. Why did you have any doubts?"

Together they got back into the boat, and the storm died away completely. The disciples knelt down and worshiped Jesus. "You truly are the Son of God," they said.

JESUS HEALS PEOPLE

Matthew 8 & 9, Mark 2, 5, & 10, Luke 5, 8, & 18

Once, when Jesus was on his way to Jerusalem, he heard a loud voice crying his name. It belonged to a blind beggar who had asked people in the crowd what all the fuss was about. "Why, Jesus of Nazareth is passing by," they told him, and the minute he heard this he yelled at the top of his voice, "Jesus, Son of David, have mercy on me!"

Those at the front of the crowd ordered him to be quiet, but he only shouted more loudly: "Son of David, have mercy on me!"

Jesus stopped and commanded those nearby to bring the man to him. His name was Bartimaeus. "What do you want me to do for you?" he asked.

"Lord, let me see," the poor man pleaded.

"Receive your sight," Jesus told him. "Your faith has healed you." At once the man could see, and he followed Jesus, glorifying God for the great miracle.

One woman had such great faith in Jesus that she believed he could heal her illness without even being asked. She had been bleeding for twelve years. "If I could only touch the hem of his robe," she said to herself, "I know I would be better." So she got to the front of the crowd one day, stretched out her hand and touched the hem of Jesus' robe. He turned around "Who touched me?" he asked, knowing that some power had gone out of him. The woman came forward. "It was I, Lord," she confessed.

Then his heart filled with love. "Your faith has healed you," he said. And she was better from that moment on.

Very often it was hard to get near to Jesus, because of the crowds. Once, a man

who was paralyzed was carried on a mat to a house where Jesus was preaching. When his friends saw that it was impossible to reach Jesus they climbed up onto the roof and removed some of the tiles. Then they lowered the man through the hole into the room below.

When Jesus saw their great faith he said to the sick man, "Your sins are forgiven." Then he said, "Take up your bed and walk." And that very instant the man stood on his feet, took up his mat, and went home praising God.

There was also a Roman soldier, a centurion, whose beloved servant was so ill he was going to die. This centurion had heard about Jesus too. He did not come himself, but he sent some Jewish elders to ask Jesus' help. "He is a good man," they told Jesus. "He loves our nation and he has built a synagogue for us." So Jesus went with them.

He was nearing the house when the centurion came out to meet him. "Lord," he said, "I am not worthy for you to come under my roof. Only say the word and my servant will be healed. I know what it's like to give orders. I am a man in authority myself. People do as I tell them."

Jesus was astonished at the faith of this man. "I have not found such faith as this in all Israel," he said. And when the centurion went back into his house he found his beloved servant alive and well.

JESUS AND HIS FRIENDS

Mark 14, Luke 7 & 19, John 3

Jesus had all kinds of friends. One of them was a man nobody else liked very much.

He was a tax-collector named Zacchaeus. People had to give him their hard-earned money.

But he wanted to see Jesus, just like everyone else, and one day the Lord was going through Jericho, where he lived. As usual the crowds were enormous. Here was the Son of Man who they hoped would save their nation. But Zacchaeus was a very small man, so he climbed up into a fig tree to get a good view of him. When Jesus reached the tree he looked up. "Zacchaeus," he called to him, "come down from there this minute. Today I'm coming to your house."

The people didn't like this. "Jesus is going to eat a meal with a sinful, greedy

man," they said. But Zacchaeus said, "I'm going to give away half my wealth to the poor, and if I've cheated anyone they can have four times what I owe."

And Jesus was glad. "The Son of Man came to seek and to save that which was lost," he said.

Jesus had another friend whom no one liked, a woman who had done bad things in her life. But she loved Jesus dearly.

One day, when he was eating a meal at his friend Simon's house, she came in carrying a jar of precious ointment. She began to weep bitterly because of all the things that had gone wrong in her life, and her tears fell on Jesus' tired and dusty feet. Kneeling down, she wiped them with her hair, and kissed them. Then she poured the ointment over them, and the house was filled with the sweet smell.

Jesus' host did not like what was happening. "This woman is a sinner," he muttered to himself.

But Jesus said, "Simon, when I entered your house you gave me no water for my feet, but this woman wet them with her tears. You gave me no kiss, but she kissed my feet. And she has poured perfume on them, while you gave me no oil for my head. This is a woman who has sinned much, but who has also loved much."

Jesus turned to the woman and said, "Your faith has saved you. Go in peace."

A man named Nicodemus stole away one night to visit Jesus. He was one of the Pharisees, the religious teachers and leaders, and he was frightened of what the others might say.

"We know you are a teacher from God," he said to Jesus. "No one could perform such miracles unless God were with him."

Jesus gave a strange answer. "To see the kingdom of God," he said, "a man must be born for a second time."

Nicodemus was puzzled. "How can a man get back inside his mother's womb and be born again?"

"You are a teacher of the people of Israel," Jesus said, "and yet you do not understand? It is through me that people can be 'born again':

"For God so loved the world, that he gave his only begotten Son, that whosoever believeth in him should not perish, but have everlasting life."

As they traveled to Jerusalem, Jesus had told his disciples that when they got there he would be put to death, but that three days later he would rise from the dead. Later, he explained, he would come back to earth and take his followers to be with him forever.

THE GOOD SAMARITAN

Luke 10

One day, a clever lawyer who had been listening to Jesus' stories decided to try to trick him. "Teacher," he asked, "what must I do if I want to live forever in God's kingdom?"

"What does it say in the Scriptures?" Jesus answered.

"It says that you must love God with all your heart, with all your soul, with all your mind, and with all your strength. After that you must love your neighbor as much as you love yourself."

"You are right," Jesus told him. "Do this and you will have everlasting life."

But the lawyer wasn't satisfied. "Who is my neighbor?" was his next question.

And Jesus told this story.

There was once a man traveling from Jerusalem to Jericho, and on a lonely stretch of road some robbers attacked him. They stripped him, beat him up, and went off leaving him half dead.

Eventually a Samaritan rode up. Now Samaritans despised Jews, so this was someone you wouldn't expect to be any help at all. But when he saw the man, pity filled his heart. He went straight over to him, poured oil and wine onto his wounds, and bandaged them up. Then he lifted the man onto his own donkey and took him to the nearest inn where he looked after him all night.

In the morning the Samaritan took out his purse and gave the innkeeper some money. "Take care of him," he said, "and if you spend any more than this, I'll pay you when I come back."

Now as it happened a priest soon came along the same stretch of road. But when he saw the poor man lying there, he simply crossed over to the other side. Some time later another priest, a Levite this time, also came walking along. He did exactly the same thing, just crossed the road and continued on his way.

At the end of the story Jesus asked, "Now which of these three people was 'neighbor' to the man who fell among thieves?"

"The one who showed mercy to him," the clever lawyer replied.

"Then go and do the same," said Jesus.

Mary, Martha, and Lazarus

Luke 10, John 11

Among Jesus' many friends were two sisters and a brother. Their names were Mary, Martha, and Lazarus. Martha was in charge of the house. She was a busy person and always seemed to have too much to do. Mary loved listening to Jesus. She would curl up at his feet and hear his stories. This annoyed Martha. One day she came to Jesus and said, "Lord, don't you see how busy I am? Don't you care? Get Mary to help me."

"Martha, Martha," Jesus said gently. "You are worried about many things, but one thing is more important than any of them, and Mary has chosen it. It must not be taken away from her."

Much later, near the time when Jesus knew he was going to suffer and die, he was told that Lazarus was very ill. "He has fallen asleep," he said, but he meant that Lazarus was dead already. "Let us go to him," he told his disciples. So they went out to Bethany, where the family lived. Lazarus had already been in his tomb for four days when Jesus came. "Lord, if you had only been here my brother would not have died," Martha said, coming out to meet him.

"He will rise again," Jesus told her. "I am the resurrection and the life. Whoever believes in me will not die. Do you believe this, Martha?"

She said, "Yes, Lord. I believe you are Christ, the Son of God."

Then Mary came out, saying the same as her sister. "If only you had been here he would not have died," and she wept so bitterly that Jesus was moved with deep compassion. When they showed him where Lazarus had been laid in his tomb, he wept with her.

"See how he loved him," some of the mourners said. But others murmured, "If he could open the eyes of the blind, couldn't he have kept this man from dying?"

Lazarus had been put in a rocky tomb and the entrance was sealed with a stone. "Take it away," Jesus commanded.

"But Lord," Martha said, "the body has been there for four days. There will be an awful smell."

"Did I not tell you that, if you believed, you would see God's glory?" he told her. So they rolled away the stone and Jesus cried, "Lazarus, come out." As they watched, Lazarus walked out of his tomb, still wrapped in grave clothes and with a cloth around his face. He was alive.

"Take the grave clothes off him and let him go," Jesus said.

This was a great miracle, but Jesus had enemies, and now they were even more afraid of what he might do next. So they got together to plot against him.

JESUS RIDES INTO JERUSALEM

Matthew 21, Mark 11, Luke 19, John 12,
Zechariah 9, Isaiah 56, Psalm 8

The time had come for Jesus to suffer and to die. He knew that terrible things were going to happen to him in Jerusalem. But first there was a moment of great rejoicing. He entered the city as a king.

Jesus sent his disciples ahead of him to fetch a donkey and her foal. "If anyone asks you what you are doing," he said, "tell them the Lord has need of them." And so the ancient saying of the prophet Zechariah was fulfilled:

"Behold, thy King cometh unto thee, meek, and sitting upon an ass."

So the disciples brought the donkey and her foal, and spread their clothes over the donkey's back, so that Jesus could

ride. A huge crowd of pilgrims, visiting the city for Passover, gathered by the roadside. Some spread out their cloaks on the ground, while others cut branches from the palm trees and put those down instead, as a royal welcome. When Jesus rode by a great shout went up: "Hosanna to the Son of David! Blessed is he who comes in the name of the Lord!"

"Who is this man?" people muttered. They had never seen anything like it before.

"Jesus of Nazareth, the prophet from Galilee," the crowds told them.

When Jesus reached the temple he became angry. It was full of people, all busy making money. They weren't worshiping God at all. And he drove them out, tipping over the counters of the money changers, and of the people who sold doves for sacrifices. "The Scriptures say this," he told them: *My house shall be called the house of prayer.* But you have turned it into a den of thieves."

The important people of the city, the chief priests and the teachers of the law, were watching Jesus very carefully. They knew people loved him; such a man was dangerous. When they heard the little children shouting, "Hosanna to the Son of David!" they didn't like it, not in front of the temple.

"Have you heard what these children are shouting?" they said indignantly.

"Yes," Jesus told them, "and do you not know what it says in the Scriptures?

"Out of the mouth of babes and sucklings thou hast perfected praise."

THE LAST SUPPER

Matthew 26, Mark 14, Luke 22, John 13

The Passover was drawing near. Everyone was busy, getting ready. But the chief priests and elders in Jerusalem were thinking up some way of trapping Jesus, and of having him put to death. They were afraid he might become too powerful, the people loved him so.

Their chance came with Judas Iscariot, one of the twelve disciples. The devil entered his heart, and he went to talk to the authorities about how he might deliver his master into their hands. Between them they worked out a plan and Judas agreed to betray Jesus in exchange for thirty pieces of silver.

Meanwhile, Peter and John were sent into the city to prepare for the Passover meal. "You will meet a man carrying a jar of water," Jesus told them. "Follow him, and when he reaches a certain house go in and say to the owner, 'Where is your guest room?' It is there that we will eat the Passover meal together."

Soon, Jesus and his twelve disciples were sitting at the table. "I have longed to eat this meal with you," he told them, "before I suffer. And I tell you this, I shall not eat bread or wine again until I do so in the kingdom of God."

While the food was being made ready Jesus got up from the table, wrapped a towel around himself, and began to wash the disciples' feet.

Peter did not understand. "You must not do this, Lord," he said.

But Jesus went to each one in turn, washing away the dust and drying their feet with the towel. "You call me 'Teacher' and 'Lord,'" he said, "and that is what I am. But I am setting you an example. I have washed your feet, and now you must wash one another's feet."

Then he gave thanks to God, broke the bread into pieces, and gave it to the disciples, saying, "This is my body." In the same way he took the cup of wine, gave it to them, and said, "This is my blood of the new covenant which will be poured out for many, so that their sins might be forgiven. Whenever you meet for this meal, do this in remembrance of me."

Then he said, "One of you sitting here will betray me." The disciples looked at one another. "Is it I, Lord? Is it I?" they whispered.

"It is the one who dips his bread into the bowl with me," Jesus answered. "It would be better for that man if he had never been born."

He knew also that the disciples would be afraid when the enemy closed in upon them, and that they would desert him. "I will never leave you, Lord," Peter said stoutly. "I will follow you to the end."

"Before the cock crows you will deny me three times," Jesus told him. Then they sang a hymn together, and went up onto the Mount of Olives.

JESUS IS ARRESTED IN THE GARDEN OF GETHSEMANE

Matthew 26, Mark 14, Luke 22, John 18

When Jesus and his disciples reached the Mount of Olives they went into the Garden of Gethsemane. He told them to keep watch, while he went away by himself to pray.

When he was alone a great agony came upon him. "Let this cup of suffering pass from me, Father," he prayed. And his sweat was like great drops of blood, falling onto the ground. Then he said, "But your will be done, not mine."

It was very late now, and one by one the disciples all fell asleep. "Could you not stay awake for a single hour?" he asked them, when he came back and found them all lying on the ground; then he returned to his prayers. But the second time he came back, and the third, he found them fast asleep as before. "Still sleeping?" he said to them as they got up, heavy-eyed, not knowing what to say. "Come. Get yourselves ready. The traitor is here." People were making their way through the darkness with lanterns, looking for Jesus.

Up they came, led by Judas, the disciple

who had betrayed him for thirty pieces of silver. They were all armed with swords and clubs, as if Jesus were some kind of robber. Judas had arranged a secret sign, to show them whom to arrest. "I will kiss him," he said.

"Hail, Master," he called, putting his arms around Jesus, and they immediately closed in and grabbed him.

"Do you betray the Son of Man with a kiss?" Jesus asked Judas Iscariot. Then the rest of the disciples ran off in terror, and Jesus was taken away to Caiaphas, the high priest. Only Peter stayed, following at a safe distance, to see what was going to happen.

He sat in the courtyard, warming himself by the fire there, while they asked Jesus all kinds of questions in an attempt to trick him. But Peter noticed that his master hardly answered a word. While they were questioning Jesus they spat at him and struck him across the face.

A maid came up to Peter and said, "You were one of Jesus' twelve friends, weren't you?" But Peter shook his head.

"I'm sure this man was with Jesus of Nazareth," she told the people standing by. But Peter swore that he was not.

"Yes, you were," they all said. "We can tell from the way you speak."

"I do not know the man!" Peter said savagely. And immediately the cock crowed.

Then Jesus turned around, and looked at Peter, and Peter remembered what had been said before they came to the Garden of Gethsemane, that before the cock crowed he would deny Jesus three times. And he went out and wept bitterly.

JESUS ON TRIAL

Matthew 27, Mark 15, Luke 23, John 18–19, Isaiah 53

The high priest, Caiaphas, and the rulers of the temple decided that Jesus must die. So they dragged him in front of Pontius Pilate, the Roman governor who was in charge of Jerusalem and of the surrounding lands. "Are you the king of the Jews?" he asked.

"You say that I am," Jesus answered. But he did not answer the charges against him.

Now at that time it was the custom for the governor to set one of his prisoners free during the feast of Passover. The people were allowed to choose who it should be. Pilate asked them if they wanted Jesus to be set free. But they asked instead for Barabbas, a rebel and a murderer.

While Pilate was discussing it with them, his wife sent him a message. "Have nothing to do with that innocent man Jesus," she said. "In my dreams last night I was deeply troubled because of him."

But the mob who had brought Jesus to the governor were determined to have him killed. "Let him be crucified," they all shouted.

"Why? What wrong has he done?" Pilate asked them. But they just shouted, "Crucify him! Crucify him!" louder and louder.

Then Pontius Pilate sent for a basin of water, and in front of them all he washed his hands. "I am innocent of this man's blood," he said. "He has done no harm at all." But he still let Barabbas go free, and Jesus was sent away.

Now it was the turn of the Roman

soldiers. To mock Jesus they made him wear a kingly robe of rich purple, pushed a crown of thorns down onto his head, and put a cane in his hand, pretending it was a royal scepter. Then they hit him and jeered at him, spitting on him and laughing, until the time had come for him to be taken out and crucified.

And so the words of the prophet Isaiah came true:

He was despised and rejected by men,
a man of sorrows, and familiar with suffering.
Like one from whom men hide their faces
he was despised, and we esteemed him not.

Surely he took up our infirmities
and carried our sorrows,
yet we considered him stricken by God,
smitten by him, and afflicted.
But he was pierced for our transgressions,
he was crushed for our iniquities;
the punishment that brought us peace was upon
*   him,*
and by his wounds we are healed.

JESUS IS CRUCIFIED

Matthew 27, Mark 15, Luke 23, John 19, Psalm 22

The place where Jesus was to be put to death was called Golgotha, which means "the place of the skull." The custom was for each man to carry his own cross, but Jesus stumbled and fell, so a man named Simon of Cyrene was called out from the crowd and forced to carry it for him.

As they nailed Jesus to the cross he prayed, "Father, forgive them. They do not know what they are doing."

Then the soldiers sat at the foot of the cross, arguing about who should have Jesus' robe, a garment without a seam, woven all in one piece. When no one could agree, they cast lots for it. A psalm had long ago described this:

They parted my raiment among them, and for my vesture they did cast lots.

Over Jesus' head they put up a sign: "The king of the Jews." People did not like this, and they said to Pontius Pilate, who had ordered it to be put there, "No, you must write that he *said* he was the king of the Jews."

"What I have written I have written," Pilate told them.

Two robbers were crucified with Jesus, one on his left hand and the other on his right. One hurled insults at him. "If you really are the Christ," he said, "save yourself, and save us too."

But the second robber rebuked the first. "Do you not fear God?" he said. "You got the same sentence as he did. So did I, and we both deserved it. But this man has done nothing wrong at all." Then he said, "Lord Jesus, remember me when you come into your kingdom."

"Today you shall be with me in Paradise," Jesus told him.

Many people stood around the foot of the cross as Jesus hung there. One of them was his mother, Mary. She was with John, the disciple Jesus especially loved. "Here is your son," he said to Mary, and to John, "Here is your mother." And from that day John took her into his own home and looked after her.

Those who passed by mocked Jesus. "He saved others," they jeered, "but he cannot save himself. Let us see if his God will help him now."

And a great darkness covered the land, from the sixth hour to the ninth. From the cross Jesus cried out with a loud voice: "*Eloi, Eloi, lama sabachthani?*" which means "My God, my God, why have you forsaken me?"

"He is calling on Elijah for help," they said, and somebody got a sponge, soaked it in vinegar and held it up to his mouth on a stick to relieve his thirst.

JESUS RISES FROM THE DEAD

Matthew 27–28, Mark 15–16, Luke 23–24, John 19–20

Before Jesus was taken down from the cross, a soldier pierced his side with a spear. Blood trickled down, and they knew he was dead. When evening came a rich man named Joseph, who was from Arimathea and had been a follower of Jesus, went to Pontius Pilate and asked if he could have the Lord's body. It was given to him, and he took it away, wrapped it in clean fresh linen, and laid it in a tomb cut out of the rock. Then he rolled a huge stone across the entrance, and went away. Mary Magdalen and Mary the mother of James sat watching.

As Jesus died he said, "Father, into your hands I commit my spirit." In the temple the curtain that shut off the Most Holy Place was split in two, from top to bottom, and the earth shook.

When the Roman officer who kept watch saw what had happened he was filled with wonder. "Truly," he said to himself, "this man was the Son of God."

Meanwhile, the men who had had Jesus put to death went to Pontius Pilate themselves. "Sir," they said, "when he was alive that liar Jesus of Nazareth claimed that three days after his execution he would rise from the dead. You ought to make sure the tomb is properly guarded, just in case his disciples steal the body and then tell people he has risen."

When the two women arrived, they saw the stone rolled back from the tomb and the angel sitting there. "Do not be afraid," the angel said. "I know you are looking for Jesus, who was crucified. He is not here, he has risen, just as he promised. Look, this is where his body lay. Now go quickly and tell his disciples that he has indeed risen from the dead and

"You may have some soldiers," Pontius Pilate told them. "Go and make the place as secure as you can." So they went off to the tomb, sealed the stone all around and set a guard to keep watch.

Early in the morning of the third day the two Marys went back to see Jesus' grave. Before they arrived, there was a tremendous earthquake, and an angel came down from heaven. His face was like lightning and his robes were as white as snow. When the guards saw him, they shook in terror and fell down, fainting.

gone on ahead into Galilee. You will see him there. This is the message I was sent to give you."

Still nervous, but with great joy in their hearts, the women hurried away from the tomb and ran to find the disciples. Suddenly Jesus met them on the path. He greeted them and they fell down before him, and clasped his feet.

"Do not be afraid," he told them, "but tell my friends that they must go to Galilee. They will see me there."

JESUS MEETS HIS DISCIPLES AGAIN

Matthew 27–28, Mark 16, Luke 24, John 20

The day Jesus appeared to the two Marys and spoke to them, two more of his followers were walking to a village called Emmaus, a place about seven miles from Jerusalem. As they talked about all that had happened, Jesus himself appeared and walked along with them, but they did not realize who it was.

He said, "What are you talking about?"

The two disciples looked sad. "Are you a stranger in Jerusalem?" they asked him. "Haven't you heard about Jesus of Nazareth? He was a great and mighty prophet, but the chief priests have had him put to death. He was our hope. We thought he was going to save Israel. And now some women we know have amazed us. They said that his tomb was empty and that an angel had told them he had risen from the dead. When our friends went to see for themselves he wasn't there."

Then Jesus chided them. "How foolish you are," he said, "and how slow to believe all that the Scriptures have told you. Did not Christ have to suffer all this, and then enter his glory?" And as they

144

walked along he explained all the places in Scripture that talked about Christ, going right back to Moses and the prophets.

When they reached Emmaus Jesus seemed to want to walk farther, but it was getting late. The two disciples persuaded him to stay, so he ate a meal with them; and it was when he broke the bread and blessed it that they realized who it was.

Suddenly Jesus disappeared, but the two men were filled with joy. "Do you remember how our hearts burned within us as he walked along the road with us?" one said to the other.

There were only eleven disciples now. Judas Iscariot, who had betrayed Jesus, was dead. He had hanged himself in remorse at the terrible thing he had done. The eleven men were frightened that people might attack them because they were faithful to Jesus, so they had to meet together secretly, in a locked room.

Into this room came Jesus. Locks and bolts did not stand in his way. "Peace be with you," he said, and he showed them where the nails had been driven into his hands and feet. They were overjoyed to see him. Then he breathed on them and gave them the power of the Holy Spirit.

Jesus had risen from the dead, but he was not a ghost. They could feel him and touch him. He even took a piece of roasted fish and ate it in front of them.

Thomas, one of the eleven disciples, was not there that day. When the others told him what had happened he refused to believe a word of it. "Unless I see the marks of the nails for myself," he said, "and put my hand into his side, where the soldiers pierced it, I will not believe."

Jesus came back to talk to Thomas. "Put your finger into the wounds here in my hands," he said. "Thrust your hand into my side. Do not doubt anymore, just believe."

Thomas sank to his knees. "My Lord and my God," he whispered.

"You believe because you have seen me for yourself," Jesus told him. "Blessed are those who do not see, and yet believe."

Later, when they were all together on a mountain in Galilee, Jesus gave them a very special command. "Go out and find disciples in all nations of the earth," he said. "Through my power baptize them in the name of the Father and the Son and the Holy Spirit. And teach them to follow everything that I have taught you.

"And lo, I am with you always, even unto the end of the world."

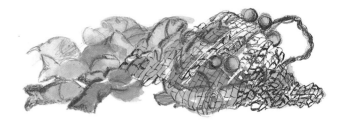

PETER'S LOVE FOR JESUS

John 21, Acts 1

In the forty days after Jesus rose from the dead, he appeared to his disciples many times.

One day some of them went fishing in a boat on the Sea of Galilee. Peter and Nathaniel were there, doubting Thomas, the two sons of Zebedee, and one or two others. They labored all through the night, but when morning came they hadn't caught a single fish.

Someone stood watching on the shore. It was Jesus, but at first they did not recognize him. "Friends," he called, "don't you have any fish?"

"No," they shouted back.

So he told them to cast their net on the right side of the boat, and it soon bulged with fish, so many that at first they could not drag it to land.

Then John, the disciple so beloved of Jesus, said, "It is the Lord!" The minute he heard this, Peter jumped into the water and swam to shore. The rest followed behind, towing the net full of fish. On the beach, a fire of coals was burning, and there was bread to eat.

"Come and have breakfast," Jesus said to them, and he shared out the bread and the fish.

When the meal was over he turned to Peter, the disciple who had been so afraid that he had denied three times over that he'd ever known Jesus. "Do you love me more than these others?" the Lord asked him now.

"Yes, Lord, you know I love you," Peter answered.

"Then feed my lambs," said Jesus.

"Peter, do you truly love me?" he asked again.

The answer was the same. "Lord, you know I love you."

"Then look after my sheep."

When Jesus asked his question a third time Peter was hurt. "Lord," he said, "you know everything. And you know I love you."

"Then feed my sheep," Jesus repeated. And he added, "When you were a young man you dressed yourself and went wherever you had a mind to go. But a time will come when you will stretch out your hands and someone else will dress you, and lead you where you do not want to go." Jesus said this knowing Peter would one day die on a cross and glorify God.

The very last time Jesus saw his disciples on earth, he told them to stay in Jerusalem because God the Father was going to give them a special gift. "John baptized with water," he said, "but soon you will be baptized with the Holy Spirit, and then you will be witnesses to me all over the earth." After he had said this he was lifted upward and a cloud hid him from their sight.

They stood there bewildered, staring up into the sky. Then two men dressed all in white appeared to them. "Men of Galilee," they said, "why do you gaze up to heaven? This same Jesus, who has been taken away from you, is going to come back. He will return in the same way that you have seen him go."

Jesus did many other things as well. If every one of them were written down, even the whole world would not have room for the books that would be written.

How the Holy Spirit Came at Pentecost

Acts 2

On the day of Pentecost (a Jewish feast day, called Shavuot, at the beginning of harvest) all the disciples were together, including Matthias, who had been chosen to take the place of Judas Iscariot. Suddenly there was the noise of a great wind blowing, a wind so powerful that it seemed to fill the house they sat in. Then they saw a fire which, as they watched, seemed to become separate tongues of flame, and the tongues rested on each one of them. They were all filled with the Holy Spirit, and they began to speak in different languages.

The noise drew a large crowd. The people were amazed at what they heard. "Aren't these men from Galilee?" they said. "And yet we can hear them speak in our own language. Some of us are Parthians, others Medes and Elamites, but they speak so that we can all understand. It is in our own tongues that they declare the marvels of God. What does this mean?"

"I am Jesus, the one you persecute," said the voice. "Get up now and go into the city. Someone will tell you what to do next."

The men with Saul saw the light and heard the voice but they did not understand what was being said. Saul staggered to his feet and found that he was blind. So they took his hand and guided him to Damascus where he found lodgings on a street called "Straight." He ate and drank nothing at all for three days.

In the city there was a believer named Ananias. The Lord spoke to him in a dream. "Go to Straight Street," he said, "and ask for Saul, from Tarsus. He knows that a man named Ananias is going to come and give him back his sight."

Ananias was uncertain. "Lord," he said, "this man Saul has done terrible things to those who believe in you. He has come here to round up your followers."

"Go," the Lord commanded. "He is the instrument I have chosen to carry my name both to Jews and to Gentiles.

Then Ananias did as he was told, found Saul, and laid his hands over his eyes, saying, "Brother Saul, it was Jesus who appeared to you on the road to Damascus. He has sent me so that you may recover your sight and be filled with the Holy Spirit."

Suddenly Saul found he could see again. They baptized him then and there; he took food and his strength came back to him.

PETER AND PAUL

Acts 10–12, 17

Peter traveled around the country healing and preaching, and lodged at last in the port of Joppa, with a tanner named Simon.

At this time there was a Roman centurion named Cornelius. He was a good man, someone who prayed hard, and an angel came to him in a dream, telling him to send servants to Joppa to bring back Peter. Cornelius did not hesitate, and three men were sent at once to the coast, to the house of Simon the tanner.

Meanwhile, Peter was up on the rooftop, praying. He was hungry and lightheaded, and he fell into a trance. In a dream he saw a great sheet being let down to earth. It was full of animals, birds, and reptiles, and the four-legged animals Jews were not allowed to eat. But a voice was saying, "Peter, get up and eat."

Peter said, "I can't. I cannot eat anything unclean."

"Nothing that God has made is unclean," answered the voice.

This happened three times, and while Peter was wondering what on earth it meant, Cornelius's servants arrived. He went back with them to Caesarea, and there the centurion greeted him by falling at his feet.

"Stand up," Peter told him. "I'm only a man, like you." And he explained that God did not have any favorites, but accepted men from all nations, so long as they did what was right. That was the meaning of his strange dream. The good news about Jesus was not only for Jews like Peter, it was for Cornelius and his family. It was for everyone.

But Peter was in danger. King Herod (the grandson of the Herod who had tried to kill the baby Jesus) was on the throne, and he wanted to harm the followers of Jesus. He had already executed James, the brother of John. Now he seized Peter too and flung him in prison. But Peter's friends prayed for him.

153

Like Peter, Saul (now renamed Paul) was going to many cities preaching the good news of Jesus. In Lystra he healed a crippled man, and the people were amazed. They thought Paul and his friend Barnabas must be two of their own gods, Hermes and Zeus in human form. So they called them by these names and started to worship them. Paul had to stop them. "We are only human beings," he said. "But we bring you marvelous news. We want you to turn from your idols and worship the God who loves you."

The night before his trial he was fast asleep. He was chained up, and there were guards on each side of him, with more at the door. Suddenly an angel appeared. He struck him on the side and woke him. "Get up," he said, and immediately Peter's chains fell off his wrists. Then the angel told him to put on his cloak and his sandals, and in a trance Peter followed him out of the prison. They walked past the first guard, then past the second. Then the iron gate of the prison opened of its own accord and they passed through into the city.

At the end of the first street the angel disappeared. Peter came around from his trance, knowing that God had saved him from the clutches of Herod.

Athens too was full of idols. Paul was fearless and preached the good news of Jesus Christ there. "You are very religious," he said. "I keep seeing altars that say, 'To the unknown god.' I have to tell you that God is not 'unknown.' In God we live and move and have our being. We are his children. He is not like a creature made from silver or gold. One day he will judge the world through Jesus Christ, whom he raised from the dead."

PAUL'S LETTERS TO THE CHURCHES

Romans 8, Psalm 44, 1 Corinthians 13, Galatians 5, Ephesians 3

Paul was a great traveler, and wherever he went he wrote letters, encouraging those who had turned to Christ.

To the church in Rome he wrote this:

Who shall separate us from the love of Christ? Shall trouble or hardship or persecution or famine or nakedness or danger or sword? As it is written: "For your sake we face death all day long; we are considered as sheep to be slaughtered."

No, in all these things we are more than conquerors through him who loved us. For I am convinced that neither death nor life, neither angels nor demons, neither the present nor the future, nor any powers, neither height nor depth, nor anything else in all creation, will be able to separate us from the love of God that is in Christ Jesus our Lord.

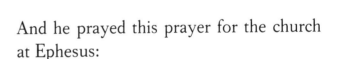

He told the people at Corinth that they must love one another more:

Love is patient, love is kind. It does not envy, it does not boast, it is not proud. It is not rude, it is not self-seeking, it is not easily angered, it keeps no record of wrongs. Love does not delight in evil but rejoices with the truth. It

always protects, always trusts, always hopes, always perseveres.

Love never fails...

And now these three remain: faith, hope, and love. But the greatest of these is love.

To the church in Galatia he talked of the Holy Spirit:

But the fruit of the Spirit is love, joy, peace, patience, kindness, goodness, faithfulness, gentleness, and self-control. Against such things there is no law.

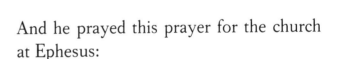

And he prayed this prayer for the church at Ephesus:

I kneel before the Father, from whom his whole family in earth and heaven derives its name. I pray that out of his glorious riches he may strengthen you with power through his Spirit in your inner being, so that Christ may dwell in your hearts through faith. And I pray that you, being rooted and established in love, may have power, together with all the saints, to grasp how wide and long and high and deep is the love of Christ, and to know this love that surpasses knowledge – that you may be filled to the measure of all the fullness of God.

REVELATION

Revelation 1, 21, & 22

God sent his angel to his servant John, to show people what would take place in the future, and this is what John wrote down:

Grace and peace to you from God the Father and from his son Jesus Christ. To him be glory and power, forever and ever!

"I am Alpha and Omega," says the Lord God, "the one who is, and was, and is to come."

I, John, was on the island of Patmos on the Lord's Day when I heard a great voice behind me, like the sound of a trumpet, ordering me to write down what I saw on a scroll and send it out to the seven churches of Asia.

This is what I saw: seven golden lampstands and someone like the Son of Man with a robe that touched his feet and a golden girdle. His head and his hair were like wool, as white as snow, and his eyes blazed fire. His feet glowed like bronze in a furnace and his voice sounded like the rushing of waters. In his right hand there were seven stars, and a double-edged sword came out of his mouth. His face shone like the sun in all its glory.

I fell at his feet, as if dead, but he put his right hand on me and said, "Do not be afraid. I am the First and the Last. I, who was dead, am alive, forever and ever, and I hold the keys of death and hell. So write down all you see. The seven stars are the angels of the seven churches, and the seven lampstands are the churches themselves."

Then I saw a new heaven and a new earth, for the first heaven and the first earth had passed away, and there was no more sea. And I saw the new Jerusalem coming down from heaven, from God, dressed as a bride would be dressed for her